The Non-Trivial TRIVIA Book

Other Books from Indus Publishing Corporation

The Family Guide to Diseases *In Plain English*

Control Yourself
*Learn how to control anger, stress, and fear and
remain happy forever*

The Complete Guide to Foreign Medical Schools

The Non-Trivial TRIVIA Book

by

Nilanjan Sen

  **Indus Publishing Corporation**

Wayland · New York

Indus Publishing Corporation
7052 Pokey Moonshine
Wayland, NY 14572
Fax: 716-728-9756

Limits of Liability and Disclaimer of Warranty:
The author and publisher have used their best efforts in preparing this book
and make no warranty of any kind, expressed or implied, with regard to the
instructions and suggestions contained herein. This book is only intended
to be used as a reference.

ISBN: 1-890838-02-0
Library of Congress: 97-093662

Credits:

The images used herein were obtained from IMSI's MasterClips Collection,
1895 Francisco Blvd. East, San Rafael, CA 94901-5506, USA.

Additional images under license from Nova Development Corporation,
USA.

Cover Design: Linda Ann Scura

Manufactured in the United States of America
3 2 1

Table of Contents

Introduction

Knowledge is power.
— Hobbes, *Leviathan*

Easy to understand, fun to use, this book is a handy mini-encyclopedia of general knowledge for anyone who wants to be informed. Hundreds of trivia questions have been grouped into five easy-to-identify categories – *geography, history, literature, science, and general topics.* You will also find brain teasers, crossword puzzles, word searches and more for your enjoyment in this book.

So gather your family and friends for hours of trivia and fun.

Start your brain cells *NOW!*

Geography

Questions

Incredible *but* True...

There are eight towns in the United States named ROME.

One-sixth of the land area of the Earth is found within the borders of Russia.

There is no place in England that is more than 75 miles from the sea.

There is a road in Canada that runs for a distance of nearly 1,100 miles.

1. Which is the world's largest ocean and who named it?

2. What is the capital of Ghana?

3. In which European country is the guilder the official currency?

4. What is the deepest point in the Indian Ocean?

5. What is the capital of Norway?

6. What is the name of the strait that divides India and Sri Lanka?

7. Which is the largest desert in the world?

8. What is Germany's second largest city?

PERU

Peru is located on the Pacific coast of South America. It is approximately 497,000 square miles in area. Peru's neighbors include Bolivia, Brazil, Chile, Colombia, and Ecuador.

Peru's primary languages are Spanish and Quechua. More than 90% of Peruvians are Roman Catholics.

The major industries of Peru are fishing, mineral processing, and textiles. The Peruvian GNP is approximately $70 billion dollars.

9. Which country is called the "Land of the White Elephant?"

10. Which is the longest river the world?

11. Which is the most densely populated continent in the world?

12. On which river is the city of Rome situated?

13. Which country is known as the "Land of Morning Calm?"

14. What is the capital of Peru?

15. Which is the largest freshwater lake in the world when measured by area?

16. Where is the Straits of Magellan?

17. Who discovered Tasmania?

18. Which continent is the home of the Bantu people?

19. What is the difference in time between each degree of longitude?

20. Which city is sometimes referred to as the "Queen of the Adriatic?"

21. Which is the world's largest delta formed by two rivers?

22. Which is the deepest lake in the world?

23. Which is the longest strait in the world?

24. In which part of the world is the River Snake located?

25. What is the capital of New Zealand and after whom was it named?

26. Which is the largest gulf in the world?

27. Which is the world's largest peninsula?

28. What are isobars?

29. Which is the longest river in Asia?

30. What was the capital of England before London?

31. Which great river in Australia is the longest tributary of the River Murray?

32. Which one of the Great Lakes is the only one that lies entirely within the United States?

33. In which country would one travel along the Gota Canal?

34. Which city is farthest north — Berlin, London or Warsaw?

35. On which in Africa river is the Victoria Falls?

36. Name the French engineer who successfully constructed the Suez Canal but failed with the Panama Canal.

37. Which city is farthest north — Beijing, Madrid, New York or Rome?

38. Between which two countries does the Pyrenees mountain range lie?

39. Which city is said to be the oldest capital in the world?

40. Which port stands at the mouth of the River Seine in France?

41. Which two countries are separated by the Gulf of Aqaba?

42. Which sea does a ship enter if it passes through Gulf of Suez and the Strait of Jubal?

43. Which are the two longest rivers in Europe?

44. In which country are the Vosges ranges?

45. Which is the largest city in Africa?

46. What country consists of North Island, South Island and Stewart Island?

47. Which countries are divided by the 49th Parallel?

48. In which country do the Ashanti people live?

49. Which country lies between Algeria and Libya?

50. Where is Table Mountain?

51. Which one of these capitals is not a port — Amsterdam, Athens, Helsinki, Oslo or Stockholm?

52. Which island did Marco Polo call "Java Minor"?

53. Which peninsula contains Norway and Sweden?

54.   Which 8928 feet-high pass lies between the
            Jammu and Kashmir Valleys in India?

55.   Which is the largest of the many islands that form
            Japan?

Time Out for Brain Teasers !!!

1.   X is the father of Y, but Y is not the son of X. How is Y related to
         X?

2.   A young girl starts to walk from a certain point. She walks one
         mile towards the east then turns left and walks another mile.
         She then turns right and walks for one more mile. At the end
         of the mile, she turns south and walks another mile. How far
         is she from the point where she started?

Answers are at the bottom of the page.

56.   Which famous canal links the North Sea to the Baltic Sea?

57.   Which is the highest mountain in Australia?

58.   Which country was formerly known as Hellas and its natives as
            Hellenas?

59.   What was the former name of Malawi?

Brain Teasers ANSWERS: 1. daughter   2. 2 miles

60. In which country is the Sierra Madre range?

61. In which sea are the Balearic Islands located?

62. What is the highest peak in the Karakoram mountain range?

63. Which two countries border Lebanon?

64. Which three countries are referred to when the name "Benelux" is used?

65. What are the grassy plains in Argentina known as?

66. Zimbabwe lies on one side of the Victoria Falls. Which country lies on the other side of the Falls?

67. Three provinces form the "toe" of the "Boot" of Italy. What is this region known as?

68. In which country is the Serengeti National Park?

69. Where is the volcano Cotopaxi?

70. Where is Timbuktu?

71. To which county does Gibraltar belong?

Where Are We?

Find the following African countries: Algeria, Egypt, Ethiopia, Madagascar, Mali, Namibia, South Africa and Zaire

Your Answers:

A. _____

B. _____

C. _____

D. _____

E. _____

F. _____

G. _____

H. _____

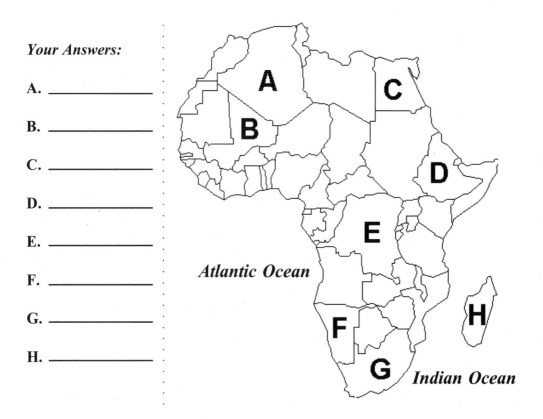

ANSWERS: **A.** *Algeria* **B.** *Mali* **C.** *Egypt* **D.** *Ethiopia* **E.** *Zaire* **F.** *Namibia* **G.** *South Africa* **H.** *Madagascar*

72. What is the source of the River Nile and who discovered it?

73. Are any of the continents entirely south of the Equator?

74. On which river are the towns of Bonn and Cologne located?

75. In which hills does the River Thames have its source?

The famous clock-tower "Big Ben" is located on the banks of River Thames in London, England.

76. On which river are the towns Luxor and Wadi Haifa?

77. Along which meridian is the International Dateline?

78. Which river makes up part of the boundaries of ten American states?

79.   Where is Kowloon Harbor?

80.   What is the name of the hot southerly wind that blows from the Sahara across Southern Italy?

81.   Where is the Kra Isthmus?

82.   What is the photosphere?

83.   The planet that orbits farthest from the sun has the same name as the God of the Underworld. What is the name of this planet?

84.   Where is Tierra del Fuego?

85.   What is the name of the country that is completely surrounded by South Africa?

86.   Which river is named after a legendary nation of female warriors?

87.   Which famous dam, completed in 1959, controls the waters of the River Zambezi in Africa?

88.   What is the present name of the island which Romans called Vectis?

89.   What is the ratio of the diameter of the Earth to that of the Sun?

90. Which planets in our solar system do not have a moon?

91. Which river rises from the springs of Mount Hermon, flows through the Sea of Gallilee and empties into the Dead Sea?

92. Which American state borders four of the Great Lakes?

93. What do the French call the English Channel?

94. How much of the Earth's surface is covered by water?

95. What is the geographical name for the upper layers of the Earth's crust?

96. Name the hot dry wind that blows from the Sahara into Egypt for about 50 days every spring.

97. To which country does Christmas Island in the Indian Ocean belong?

98. What is the name of the mineral which, under pressure, changes into marble over time?

99. Brazil is the largest South American country. Which is the smallest?

100. Which country now covers the area which was once the kingdom of Babylonia?

Nations & Flags

Match the flags on the left with the countries on the right.

Your Answers:

A.

Kenya

A. _____

B.

Brazil

B. _____

C.

United Kingdom

C. _____

D.

Nepal

D. _____

ANSWERS: *A. Nepal* **B.** *United Kingdom* **C.** *Kenya* **D.** *Brazil*

101. What is the capital of Grenada in the West Indies?

102. Gabon, Zaire, and Congo lie on the Equator in the African continent. What are the other three African countries on the Equator?

103. Where is the Coromandel Coast?

104. What is the capital of Maldives?

105. What is the oldest capital city in the Americas?

• *End of Trivia Questions* •

Did You Know???

There is 43,560 square feet in an acre.

Nike was the Greek goddess of victory.

There are eight time zones in North America.

Reading, PA is also known as the *Pretzel City*.

Rome was built on seven hills: Aventine, Caelian, Capitoline, Esquiline, Quirinal, and Viminal.

Name this famous structure.

Clues:

- The above structure is situated in a city located in Tuscany, Italy.
- It is approximately 180 feet tall.

ANSWER: *The Leaning Tower of Pisa*

Famous Icons

Match the icons on the left with the correct names on the right.

A.

Venus de Milo

Your Answers:

A. _____

B.

Marines at Iwo Jima

B. _____

C. _____

C.

Taj Mahal

ANSWERS: **A.** *Taj Mahal* **B.** *Venus De Milo*
C. *Marine at Iwo Jima*

Cross Word Puzzle
World Cities #1

Across

2. Elysee Palace
4. Charles Bridge
5. Brooklyn
7. Dam Square
11. Mother Theresa
12. Capital of Zaire

Down

1. Golden Gate Bridge
3. Sugarloaf Mountain
4. Liberty Bell
6. Antoni Gaudi's City
8. 1988 Summer Olympics
9. Capital of Syria
10. Microsoft Corporation

Word Quest
Unites States Rivers

I	C	Y	N	E	H	G	E	L	L	A	A	E	H	G
P	W	E	O	M	R	O	M	I	P	R	K	D	O	G
P	W	L	S	P	I	A	D	J	K	O	F	N	I	F
I	Y	L	D	G	O	N	W	A	N	G	W	R	H	T
S	S	O	U	H	G	T	N	A	R	V	U	D	O	S
S	U	W	H	Q	R	S	O	E	L	O	T	Y	E	Q
I	D	S	F	V	A	R	E	M	S	E	L	M	Y	R
S	N	T	Q	S	N	N	S	S	A	O	D	O	Y	Q
S	E	O	K	U	D	B	I	A	Z	C	T	K	C	K
I	E	N	M	X	E	M	X	V	N	R	C	A	Q	I
M	F	E	L	L	A	H	S	A	I	U	O	Y	J	S
G	A	L	A	B	A	M	A	N	T	S	N	A	K	E
Q	R	U	B	N	B	S	I	N	V	O	M	C	K	A
E	H	P	L	A	T	T	E	A	N	E	E	R	A	O
H	C	O	K	C	Y	K	R	H	S	A	B	A	W	S

Search for the following rivers:

Alabama	Allegheny	Arkansas	Colorado
Delaware	Green	Hudson	James
Kentucky	Minnesota	Mississippi	Missouri
Ohio	Platte	Potomac	Powder
RioGrande	Roanoke	Salmon	Savannah
Snake	Susquehanna	Trinity	Wabash
Yellowstone			

Cross Word Puzzle
World Cities #2

Across

1. Sears Tower
5. Acropolis
6. Highest Capital City
7. Changi Airport
8. Constantinople
13. CN Tower
14. Emerald Island City
15. Trevi Fountain

Down

2. The Statue of Mermaid
3. Capital of Zimbabwe
4. Holy Muslim City
9. Buckingham Palace
10. River Nile
11. Red Square
12. Narita Airport

Congratulations!

You have just completed the first group of trivia questions.

On to the next group...

History

Questions

Incredible *but* True...

An albatross may fly all day and not flap its wings once.

The only animal that sleeps on its back is the human being.

It takes over ten years for a cork tree to grow one layer of cork.

Grasshoppers have white blood.

There are 2.5 million rivets in the Eiffel Tower.

1.　When was the city of Calcutta founded?

2.　In which year was Martin Luther King, Jr. assassinated?

3.　What city in Egypt was founded by Alexander the Great?

4.　Who was Kemal Ataturk?

5.　In which year was the first atom bomb dropped?

6.　Who was the founder of Protestantism in Germany?

7.　Who founded the Chinese Republic in 1911?

8.　Name the palace built by King Louis XIV, 12 miles from Paris, which is widely regarded as one of the world's most magnificent buildings.

9.   In which century did the Industrial Revolution start in Europe?

10.   Name the Roman Emperor who ruled from 54 A.D. to 68 A.D., noted for his wickedness and cruelty.

Christopher Columbus

11.   Who was the last ruler of the Moghul Dynasty?

12.   Who was considered the most elegant of Roman orators during the first century B.C.?

13.   Name the plain in Greece which is witnessed a great victory for the Greeks over the Persians under Darius in 490 B.C.

14.   Which religion has 24 great teachers called the Tirthankars?

15.   Which Roman Emperor was the first emperor to convert to Christianity and to forbid any religious persecution of Christians in 313 A.D.?

16.   When did the French revolution start?

17.   Name the peace treaty signed at the close of World War I between the Allies and Germany.

18. What nationality was Christopher Columbus?

19. Which general came to power after the 1939 Civil War in Spain?

20. Which European monarch history ruled for the longest period of time?

21. What was the real name of Genghis Khan?

22. Which great queen is said to have visited Solomon?

23. What served as the emblem of ancient Rome?

Genghis Khan

24. Which famous world leaders atteneded the Potsdam Conference?

25. In what year was China admitted to the U.N.?

26. How many Georges have sat on the throne of England?

27. Who was the British Prime Minister when World War I was declared?

28. In which year were England and Scotland united?

29. What important event took place on December 7, 1941 during World War II?

30.   Who succeeded Colonol Nasser as President of Egypt?

31.   Who took over as Commander of the German Armed Forces after
       Hitler's death, and authorized the unconditional surrender of
       Germany in 1945?

32.   Who was the youngest monarch in British history?

33.   What was the name of Columbus' flag ship?

34.   Golda Meir became Israel's Prime Minister in 1969. Where was
       she born?

First Five Women Prime Ministers	
1. S. Bandaranaike	Sri Lanka
2. Indira Gandhi	India
3. Golda Meir	Israel
4. E. Domitien	Central African Republic
5. Margaret Thatcher	United Kingdom

35.   Which is the oldest legislative body in the world?

36.   Which family ruled France for more than 200 years?

37.   Where did Alexander the Great die?

38.   Which King of England built the Tower of London?

39.   Where did Julius Ceasar defeat Pompey?

40.   Name the Spanish soldier who conquered Mexico.

FYI   FYI   FYI   FYI

What two cities other than Pompeii were destroyed by the volcanic eruption of Mt. Vesuvius?

The volcanic eruption destroyed three cities. They were Pompeii, Herculaneum, and Stabiae. The eruption took place in A.D. 79. The buried cities were not discovered till late 1500s.

41.   In what country did the Boxer Rebellion take place in 1900?

42.   When was the Suez Canal (Egypt) opened?

43.   Of which British king was it said, "He never said a foolish thing, nor ever did a wise one"?

44.   Who was the last Roman emperor?

45.   What was the ancient name for the modern day country known as
Ethiopia?

World's Leading Explorers		
Explorer	*Nationality*	*Discovered*
Pedro Cabral	Portuguese	Brazil
Vasco Balboa	Spanish	Panama
Juan Ponce de Leon	Spanish	Florida
Hernando Cortes	Spanish	Mexico
Ferdinand Magellan	Portuguese	Straits of Magellan & Tierra del Fuego
Giovanni da Verrazano	Italian	Northern Atlantic coast of America
Francisco Pizarro	Spanish	Peru
Jacques Cartier	French	Canada
Pedro de Mendoza	Spanish	Buenos Aires
Francisco de Orellana	Spanish	River Amazon
Hernando de Soto	Spanish	River Mississippi
Sir Francis Drake	English	California Coast
Sir Walter Raleigh	English	River Orinoco
Henry Hudson	English	River Hudson
Jean Nicolet	French	Lake Michigan

46.   How long did the Great Fire of London last in 1666?

47.   Who coined the phrase "Iron Curtain"?

48.   Which famous Brit was killed at the Battle of Trafalgar?

49. What were the wars between Rome and Carthage called?

50. Where was Buddha born?

51. What were the words with which H.M. Stanley is supposed to have greeted David Livingstone when he found him in Africa?

52. What was the Spanish Armada?

53. In which year was Mohammed the Prophet born?

54. Which is the oldest national flag in existence?

55. Which family ruled Russia for more than 300 years?

56. What was the original nationality of Catherine the Great, Empress of Russia?

57. A Venezuelan revolutionary helped to liberate Bolivia. What is the name of this revolutionary?

ISLAM

Islam was founded by Mohammed around A.D. 610. Mohammed's teachings are contained in the Islamic holy book, the Koran. Muslims believe the Koran to be the word of the one God.

Islam is the second largest religion in the world. Most Muslims are members of either the Sunni or Shiite sect. The religious duty of Muslims are summed up in the "Five Pillars". They are as follows:

- The Creed: "There is no god but God, and Mohammed is the prophet of God".
- The Prayer: Muslims are expected to pray five times a day.
- Almsgiving: Muslims are expected to give alms for the support of the faith and poor.
- Fasting: Muslims are expected to fast during the daylight hours of the month of Ramadan.
- The Pilgrimage: Once in a lifetime, if possible, every Muslim is expected to make the pilgrimage to Mecca.

58. What two countries fought the Crimean War?

59. Who was the Muslim warrior who defied the Christian knights in the Third Crusade?

60. Which important organization came into being after an international conference in Geneva in 1864?

61. Which war was ended by the Treaty of Paris, signed in February, 1856?

62. Lack of which crop lead to the great Irish Faminine in 1845-47?

63. Who were the three Axis Powers in World War II?

64. Who was Catherine of Aragon?

65. What dynasty ruled China until 1911?

66. Which important international organization came into being with the Treaty of Versailles?

67. Who reportedly said that the English are a "nation of shopkeepers?"

68. Which Greek monarch was deposed in 1967?

FYI   FYI   FYI   FYI

How long was the Berlin Wall?

The wall that divided the city of Berlin into East and West Berlin ran for 26.5 miles. The wall was erected in August, 1961. It divided Berlin for 28 years before it was taken down on November 9, 1989.

69. What is the aptly named town that British philanthropists founded towards the end of 18th century as a home for freed slaves in Africa?

70. Name the three great civilizations of the ancient Americas.

71. Who was the Egyptian God of the Sun?

72. According to Virgil, who was the Trojan hero who founded the Roman nation?

73. Which two modern day countries celebrate Independence Day on August 15th?

74. Which World War II leader rode on a private train named Amerika?

75. Name the battle that resulted in the greatest number of casualties during the Civil War?

• *End of Trivia Questions* •

Time Out for Brain Teasers !!!

1. What object gets wetter as it dries?

Brain Teasers ANSWER: 1. A towel

Word Quest
Founding Fathers

N	K	K	T	U	S	D	F	J	I	C	J
V	O	Y	T	W	Y	N	E	N	J	W	N
U	T	S	E	O	I	F	I	D	J	O	J
T	E	E	L	Y	F	L	B	K	J	L	N
K	U	F	T	E	K	O	S	G	P	C	O
C	D	E	R	N	N	S	A	O	H	O	C
O	H	S	A	D	A	M	S	A	N	T	H
C	O	R	B	O	P	I	R	O	M	T	A
N	F	P	C	R	W	T	B	H	R	W	S
A	Q	W	K	E	B	H	S	T	O	N	E
H	A	L	L	B	Y	U	L	I	O	S	Q
P	Y	V	Q	F	R	T	L	G	C	G	A

Search for the following founding fathers:

Adams	Hopkins	Smith
Bartlett	Jefferson	Stone
Chase	Lee	Wilson
Floyd	Lewis	Wolcott
Franklin	Nelson	
Hall	Rodney	
Hancock	Ross	
Hart	Rush	

Literature

Questions

Incredible *but* True...

The most expensive paper in the world is a special type of hand-made Finnish writing paper priced at $8,000 per 100 sheets.

During the seven years Wordsworth was a Poet Laureate, he did not write a single poem.

Arabs have more than 1,000 different words to describe a camel.

The sentence "The quick brown fox jumps over the lazy dog" contains all 26 letters of the alphabet.

1.   What is the title of the world's longest poem?

2.   Who created the character Scarlet Pimpernel?

3.   In which of Shakespeare's plays does the character Shylock appear?

4.   Who wrote *Alice in Wonderland*?

5.   In Shakespeare's *Othello,* who was the title character's love?

6.   Who wrote the Greek epics *Illiad* and *Odyssey*?

7.   What was the real name of the author George Eliot?

8.   Who wrote *Of Human Bondage*?

9.   Who wrote *Ivanhoe*?

10. Name the French writer whose book, *The Social Contract,* was said to have inspired the French Revolution.

William Shakespeare (1564-1616)

Shakespeare was born in Stratford-upon-Avon in England. In 1582, he married Anne Hathaway. In 1585, Shakespeare traveled to London and started his literary career. His range of work is diverse. Thirty eight plays are attributed to him although there is some doubt that he wrote them all.

11. Who wrote *A Tale of Two Cities*?

12. In which poem do these lines appear: "For men may come or men may go, but I go on for ever"?

13. Who wrote *Don Quixote*?

14. Where was the first edition of the *Encyclopedia Britannica* published?

15. Shakespeare's play *Twelfth Night* is also known by another title. What is it?

16. What are the first names of the two brothers who wrote *Grimm's Fairy Tales*?

17. What was Mark Twain's real name?

18. "If music be the food of love, play on." Give the name of the play in which this line is uttered.

 *World Literature*

Match the books on the left with the authors on the right.

		Your Answers:
A. Palace Walk	Salman Rushdie England	A. _____
B. The City and the House	Rabindranath Tagore India	B. _____
C. Tieta	Marguerite Duras France	C. _____
D. Midnight's Children	Natalia Ginzburg Italy	D. _____
E. Annie John	Naguib Mahfouz Egypt	E. _____
F. Silence	Shusako Endo Japan	F. _____
G. Gitanjali	Jorge Amado Brazil	G. _____
H. India Song	Jamaica Kincaid Antigua	H. _____

Answers: A: Mahfouz B. Ginzburg C. Amado D. Rushdie E. Kincaid F. Endo G. Tagore H. Duras

Cross Word Puzzle
General

Across	Down	
1. speak	2. exhaust	58. hydrochloric _____
5. a food dish	3. Norse god of war	61. Kansas
10. an African fish	4. Ethyleneoxide	62. King Gradlon's capital
11. tone in diatonic scale	5. chocolate	63. blue grass state
12. top executive	6. sooner than expected	64. mouth
13. mishap	7. eight musicians	66. swimming event
16. measure of print (pl)	8. article (fr)	
19. eggs	9. government agency (acr)	
20. however	11. rush about	
22. largest artery	14. engineering degree	
24. mesh	15. borders Canada	
26. connection	17. goddess of fertility	
28. connecting word	18. lament	
30. stocking (Fr)	21. link	
31. stimulant	23. frenzy	
33. type tray	24. wordage	
34. Apollo's son	25. fragment	
36. continent (abbr)	27. imitate	
37. Hebrew letter	28. Houston team	
39. most deafening	29. perch	
40. superlative	31. you (sp)	
41. haw, as cattle	32. most populous state	
43. alder tree (scot)	35. pecan, cashew	
45. right (abbr)	36. ordinal number suffix	
46. Finn in Ingria	38. moving vehicle	
49. dwarf	42. officer of guard (abbr)	
51. them (singular)	43. Norwegian territory	
52. more sheltered	44. football position (acr)	
54. intestines	46. cargo vehicle	
55. three (ital)	47. frequently	
56. comprise	48. social affair	
58. Scottish oak	50. remove	
59. unbroken	51. irritate	
60. Aspen ____ Resort	52. consequently	
63. Dutch dry measure	53. borders Connecticut	
65. stitchbird	55. one tenth	
67. compositions	56. bag	
68. preparatory school	57. bite	

American Literature

Match the books on the left with the authors on the right.

A. Light in August	Toni Morrison	*Your Answers:*
		A. _____
B. The Awakening	Mary McCarthy	
		B. _____
C. The Kitchen God's Wife	Gertrude Stein	
		C. _____
D. The Company She Keeps	William Faulkner	
		D. _____
E. Humboldt's Gift	Edith Wharton	
		E. _____
F. Three Lives	Saul Bellow	
		F. _____
G. The House of Mirth	Kate Chopin	
		G. _____
H. Sula	Amy Tan	
		H. _____

Answers: A: Faulkner B. Chopin C. Tan D. McCarthy E. Bellow F. Stein G. Wharton H. Morrison

19. Name the Russian composer who wrote the music for *The Sleeping Beauty*.

20. Who is described by Shakespeare as "the noblest Roman of them all"?

21. Who wrote, "If God did not exist, it would be necessary to invent him"?

FYI   FYI   FYI   FYI

Do you know how many books Isaac Asimov has written?

Isaac Asimov is one of the most prolific contemporary writers, with over 400 books to his credit. Asimov wrote his first book, *Pebble in the Sky,* in 1950.

22. Who was the author of *Seven Pillars of Wisdom*?

23. Who is considered to be the greatest German poet?

24. Who killed Macbeth in Shakespeare's play of the same title?

25.   Which English poet is buried on the Greek Island of Skyros?

26.   In which country's mythology would the characters Isis and Osiris appear?

Ernest Hemingway

27.   Who wrote *Twenty Thousand Leagues Under the Sea* in 1870?

28.   Which was the last play written by William Shakespeare?

29.   Who was the overweight knight who suffered at the hands of Shakespeare's *Merry Wives of Windsor*?

30.   Under what name did Sir Arthur Conan Doyle write?

31.   Whose epitaph ended with the following: "I hope to see my pilot face to face when I have crossed the bar"?

32.   Who was the American-born British poet who won the Noble Prize for Literature in 1948?

33.   For which of his books did Ernest Hemingway win the Noble Prize?

34.   Which authors who started the existentialist movement in literature?

Word Game

I. *Which word, when added to the letters on the left, will form a new word?*

b

t

p

r

br

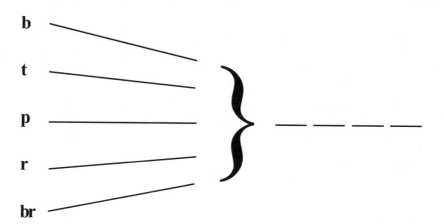

Venice, Italy

Venice is located in the eastern region of Italy. The city was built gradualy in the shallow waters of a lagoon by reinforcing the land which emerged at intervals during the ebb and flow of the tides. The Grand Canal which flows through the city is nothing other than an ancient riverbed flowing towards the sea. The famous Venetia palazzi (gorgeous multi-storied buildings), beautiful churches, and narrow streets were all created by Venetians over a period of ten centuries. Many of the palazzi and churches are a triumphant expression of the Renaissance and reflect the fact that ties Venice to this period of time.

35. Who wrote *Lord of the Flies*?

36. In *Merchant of Venice*, of what metal is used to make the casket that bears his inscription: "Who chooseth me shall get as much as he deserves"?

37. Who wrote *Gone with the Wind*?

38. Hamlet, the hero of Shakespeare's play, was a prince from which country?

39. On what day of the week did Robinson Crusoe meet his future servant and friend?

40. What are the giants in Swift's *Gulliver's Travels* called?

41. What is the title of the book that Charles Dickens began but did not live to complete?

42. Which poem by Matthew Arnold is based on a Persian national epic?

43. Who wrote the play *Pygmalion*?

44. Which father created the fictional detective Father Brown?

45. Who was King Arthur's fairy sister?

46. According to Shakespeare, to whom did Julius Caesar bequeath 75 drachmas?

All-Time Best Selling Books
1. The Bible
2. Quotations from the Works of Mao Tse-tung
3. American Spelling Book (Noah Webster)
4. The Guiness Book of World Records
5. The McGuffey Readers (William McGuffey)

47. What is Guy de Maupassant's full name and for what is he famous?

48. What is Epicurean philosophy?

49. Who created the comic strip *Dennis the Menace*?

50. What kind of bird took Sinbad the Sailor to its lair in *The Arabian Nights*?

51. For how many years did Rip Van Winkle sleep in Washington Irving's story?

52.   Who wrote a famous poem about the charge of the Light Brigade?

53.   Which famous novel by R. D. Blackmore has the subtitle *A Romance of Exmoor*?

54.   Which famous epic, 3000 lines long, written on twelve clay tablets was discovered in the library of Ashurbanipal at Nineveh?

FYI   FYI   FYI   FYI

Do you know that there are 24 Canterbury Tales?

Knights Tale	Physician's Tale
Miller's Tale	Pardoner's Tale
Reeve's Tale	Shipman's Tale
Cook's Tale	Prioress's Tale
Man of Law's Tale	Tale of Sir Thopas
Wife of Bath's Tale	Tale of Melibee
Friar's Tale	Monk's Tale
Summoner's Tale	Nun's Priest's Tale
Clerk's Tale	Second Nun's Tale
Merchant's Tale	Canon's Yeoman's Tale
Squire's Tale	Manciple's Tale
Franklin's Tale	Parson's Tale

55. Which lines of a limerick rhyme with each other?

56. Name the playwright who wrote *A Streetcar Named Desire*?

57. For what are the McWhirter twins known?

58. What is a "burletta" in literature?

59. A famous Russian novelist, Aleksy Maksimovich Pyeshkov is better known by another name. What is it?

Most Published Authors	
1. W. Shakespeare	England
2. Charles Dickens	England
3. Sir. Walter Scott	England
4. Johann Goethe	Germany
5. Aristotle	Greece

60. In literature, what is the difference between bathos and pathos?

61. In which classic English literary work is Banquo a character?

62. What is the title of the musical based on the life of the Von Trapp family?

63. The setting for D. H. Lawrence's novel *Kangaroo* was Australia. What was the setting for his novel *The Plumed Serpent*?

64. Who created the mythical hero Paul Bunyan?

65. Who is the author of the book *The Red Badge of Courage*?

66. What is Omar Khayyam's most famous work?

67. Who is the author of the book *The Count of Monte Cristo*?

68. Who is the author of the book *The Hound of Baskervilles*?

69. "East is east, west is west and never shall the twin meet." Who wrote the above sentence?

70. Who is the author of the famous literary work *Les Miserables*?

71. Who created the *Archie* comics series?

72. Who are the authors of the comics series *Spiderman*?

73. What is an "antonym"?

74. Which poet started the weekly newspaper *The Long Islander*?

75. Who wrote the 11th century Japanese novel *The Tale of Genji*?

• *End of Trivia Questions* •

FYI   FYI   FYI   FYI

Do you know the real names of the following authors?

Author	Pen Names
Mary Ann Evans	George Eliot
Hector Hugh Munro	Saki
François-Marie Arouet	Voltaire
Aleksei Peshkov	Maksim Gorki
Charles Dickens	Boz
Thomas Kennerly, Jr.	Tom Wolfe
Samuel Clemens	Mark Twain
Jean Baptiste Poquelin	Molière
Charles Lutwidge Dodgson	Lewis Carroll
William Sydney Porter	O. Henry
Marie Henri Beyle	Stendahl
Theodor Seuss Geisel	Dr. Seuss
David John M. Cornwell	John le Carré

Science

Questions

Incredible *but True...*

> There are more than 200 different viruses that can cause colds.
>
> A camel has no gall bladder.
>
> Each square inch of human skin consists of 19 million cells..
>
> The sun burns 240,000,000 tons of hydrogen gas every minute.
>
> Water dissolves more substances than any other liquid.

1. Who invented the telephone?

2. Who compiled the first logarithmic tables – *Mirifici Logarithmorum Canonis Descripto*?

3. Who discovered the electron?

4. Who discovered that malaria is carried by mosquitoes?

5. Which is the longest bone in the human body?

6. Who obtained the first patent for radio broadcasting?

7. Who invented the lightning conductor?

8. Why do we feel no pain when cutting our nails?

9.   Who invented the ball point pen?

10.   Who discovered penicillin?

11.   What do we call the science that deals with the principles of flight?

FYI   FYI   FYI   FYI

Do you know how many types of clouds there are?

According to meteorologists, there are 10 different types of clouds. They are named altocumulus, altostratus, cirrus, cirrocumulus, cirrostratus, cumulus, cumulonimbus, nimbostratus, stratus and stratocumulus.

12.   Who discovered insulin?

13.   Who put forth the modern theory of Atomic Structure?

14.   What is a catalyst?

15.   What type of mirror is used by motorists to see the road behind them?

16. Who discovered oxygen?

17. What is the difference between mass and weight?

18. What is the popular name for the gas called nitrous oxide, commonly used as an anesthetic?

19. Would you press your finger against a vein or an artery to check your pulse?

Time Out for Brain Teasers !!!

What is the missing number?

17	31	?
18	22	72

---

20. Who discovered the circulation of blood?

21. Who discovered calcium?

22.   What is the name of the first space craft to land on the moon?

23.   Which is the largest muscle in the human body?

24.   Give the exact rate of acceleration of free fall in a vacuum.

25.   Which is the smallest bone in the human body?

26.   What is the approximate internal temperature of the sun?

27.   Who discovered the Laws of Heredity?

28.   A human heart has four chambers. How many chambers are there in a frog's heart?

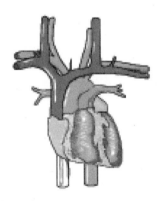

The Human Heart

The human heart is a cone shaped muscle. It is no larger in size than an adult human fist. The heart is located in the thoracic cavity, in a space between the lungs, just to the left of a bone called the sternum.

The heart has four chambers: the right atrium, the left atrium, the right ventricle and the left ventricle. The right side of the heart receives oxygen-poor blood (deoxygenated blood) from the body. It circulates deoxygenated blood to lungs where new oxygen molecules enter the blood for use by our bodily organs. The oxygen-rich blood (oxygenated blood) is then circulated from the lungs to the left side of the heart. The left side of the heart is responsible for pumping oxygenated blood throughout our body.

Test of Reasoning

How many square blocks do you see in the figure below?

Clue: By definition, all square blocks have sides that are of equal length and width.

Answer on the next page.

Test of Reasoning
Answer

There are **14** square blocks.

1	2	3
4	5	6
7	8	9

Square# 10 – the entire box

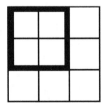 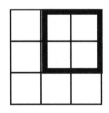 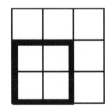 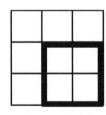

Square# 11   Square# 12   Square# 13   Square# 14

29. How many wings do butterflies, moths, and bees have?

30. What is the uppermost layer of the Earth's atmosphere called?

31. Who was the first to measure the velocity of light?

32. For what is a galvanometer used?

33. Which element makes up the primary structure of diamonds?

34. There are how many points in a mariner's compass?

35. What is Boyle's Law?

36. What is another name for vitamin B_1?

Vitamins		
Vitamin	**Importance**	**Sources**
A	Needed for good vision	carrots and liver
B1	Needed for muscle and nervous system functioning	whole grains, breads and cereals, fish
B2	Maintains healthy skin	peas, beans and low-fat milk
B3	Helps break down food	fish, potatoes and cereals
C	Plays many roles in the maintenance of cells	Tomatoes, citrus fruits and broccoli
D	Needed for healthy bones and teeth	milk, bread and cereals
E	Needed in the formation of red blood cells	fish, green vegetables and eggs
K	Needed for blood clotting	Green vegetables, fruits and potatoes

37. In physics, what name is given to the study of motion?

38. What is dilute acetic acid better known as?

FYI FYI FYI FYI

Do you know what glass is made of?

Glass is made from three fundamental components: soda or potash, lime and silica (such as sand). During the glass making process all three components are first mixed together, heated and then cooled to form transparent glass.

39. How long does it take for light to travel from the Sun to the Earth?

40. What is the medical name of the dysfunction "lockjaw"?

41. Who discovered radioactivity?

42. What is the principal mineral in marble?

43. A pain-killing drug was named after the Greek god of dreams. What was his name?

44.   What is the Telstar?

45.   What is escape velocity?

46.   Why is air removed from an electric bulb?

47.   Which instrument is used to study the spectra of radiation emitted by light sources such as stars?

48.   What is lipase?

Most Used Prescription Drugs	
1. Zantac	Ulcers
2. Vasotec	Hypertension
3. Capoten	Hypertension
4. Voltaren	Arthritis
5. Tenormin	Hypertension

49.   Which star is nearest to the Earth?

50.   What are the two other names for the Ursa Major star constellation?

51.   When a human being experiences fear, which hormone is secreted and what effect does it have?

52.   How many degrees of longitude equal one hour of time?

53.   For what is Charles Darwin famous?

54.   The most common illness in the world is the common cold. What is the most common disease?

All About Medicine

Largest Human Bones
Femur (the thighbone)
Tibia (the shinbone)
Fibula
Humerus
Ulna

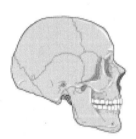

Causes of Death Worldwide	
Cause	*Rate per 100,000*
Infectious Diseases	331
Circulatory System Diseases	225
Cancer	97
Accidents	65

FYI FYI FYI FYI

The Discovery of Antibiotics

The discovery of antibiotics is one of the most important landmarks in the history of medicine. Antibiotics have greatly helped physicians in controlling infectious diseases. Antibiotics have also made surgery safer than ever before.

The first antibiotic was discovered by Alexander Fleming in 1928. He observed that when green mold was grown in culture plates containing staphylococci bacteria, the bacteria failed to grow. Although Fleming could not explain his observation at the time, some twelve years later Penicillin, the first antibiotic, was isolated.

Scientists have defined antibiotics as natural or synthesized chemicals that have the ability to curb the growth of bacteria. However, the range of their effectiveness is limited. An individual antibiotic is effective against a particular type of bacteria. Antibiotics are ineffective against all other types of microorganisms other than bacteria.

55.   What chemical element does hemoglobin contain?

56.   What are polysaccharides?

57.   Which is the only mammal that can fly?

58.   What is a scalene triangle?

59.   What is a black widow?

Panda   Platypus

60.   Which one of the following animals is not indigenous to Australia: wallaby, platypus or panda?

61.   What is a dried grape called?

62.   What gives the illusion that stars twinkle?

63.   Which glands are inflamed when you get the mumps?

64.   Where are Haversian Canals located?

65.   What gas represents 78% of atmospheric air?

66.   The shape of bacterial cells can be broadly classified into three types; Spirilla are spiral in shape, Cocci are spherical. What is the shape of Bacilli?

67.   Who invented the cash register?

68.   A botanist studies plants. What does a cytologist study?

69.   What is the normal life cycle of the common fly?

70.   Unlike the rest of the planets in our solar system, one planet rotates clockwise on its axis. Which planet is it?

71.   In a cranial injury, which part of the body is hurt?

72.   When an individual is said to suffer from dichromatic vision, what does it mean?

73.   Why do sailers have a special interest in the star Polaris?

74.   What part of the human body account for one quarter of all the

bones in the body?

75. What is the name of the scientific discipline that deals with the study of projectiles?

• *End of Trivia Questions* •

Math Power
The History of Mathematics

3500 B.C.   Egyptians develop an extensive numbering system.

2000 B.C.   Mesopotamians develop a system that can solve quadratic equations.

876 A.D.   Zero is used for the first time in mathematics in India.

1536 A.D.   Niccolo Tartaglia (Italy) solves cubic equations.

1614 A.D.   John Napier (Scotland) defines logarithms.

1637 A.D.   Rene Descartes (France) defines analytic geometry.

1654 A.D.   Blaise Pascal and Pierre de Fermat (France) state basic laws of probability.

1666 A.D.   Isaac Newton (England) reveals the invention of calculus.

1881 A.D.   Josiah Gibbs (U.S.) introduces vector analysis.

1976 A.D.   Miklos Laczkovich (Hungary) provides proof that a circle can be divided into a finite number of pieces and then reassembled into a square.

Time Out for Brain Teasers !!!

1. Mr. and Mrs. Jones have five sons and each son has one sister. How many people are there in the Jones family?

2. Six cars are lined up bumper-to-bumper. How many bumpers are actually touching each other?

Answers are at the bottom of the page.

Brain Teasers ANSWERS: 1. 8 (Mr. & Mrs. Jones+5 sons+one daughter since each son has the same sister).   2. 10

Word Quest
Famous Scientists

E	G	A	L	I	L	E	O	C	N	I	S
I	L	N	I	W	R	A	D	J	S	C	E
N	Q	O	I	N	A	M	A	R	J	I	I
S	O	S	Y	T	H	J	E	N	N	E	R
T	V	T	M	T	N	L	D	K	C	Z	U
E	Q	A	W	S	P	A	V	L	O	V	C
I	L	W	O	E	L	W	B	S	R	Y	R
N	Y	Y	K	T	N	E	T	T	A	E	I
S	R	H	O	B	U	K	D	U	S	L	C
Y	T	N	J	B	A	B	C	N	U	Y	K
Y	V	Q	X	J	F	B	D	U	E	R	F
U	I	I	M	F	I	Y	T	X	Q	M	L

Search for the following famous scientists:

Banting	Darwin	Mendel
Bohr	Einstein	Newton
Boyle	Freud	Pavlov
Crick	Galileo	Raman
Curie	Jenner	Salk
Dalton	Kepler	Watson

General Topics

Questions

Incredible *but* True…

An albatross may fly all day and not flap its wings once.

The only animal that sleeps on its back is human.

It takes over ten years for a cork tree to grow one layer of cork.

Grasshoppers have white blood.

There are 2.5 million rivets in the Eiffel Tower.

1. Which is the largest administrative building in the world?

2. Which is the world's tallest statue?

3. How many miles per hour (mph) is one knot?

4. The Library of the United Nations is named after which person?

5. In which year was the Noble Prize established?

6. Which is the fastest fish in the world?

7. Paramaribo is the capital of what country?

8. Which is the world's longest railway bridge?

9.   Name the U.S. space vehicle that made the first soft-landing on the moon on June 2, 1966.

10.   How many liters equal a gallon?

11.   Who is known as the "Shadow Prime Minister" in Britain?

"The moon, like a flower,
In heaven's high bower
With silent delight
Sits and smiles on the night."
– **BLAKE**, *Night*

12.   What is India's national flower?

13.   What is the approximate distance between the Earth and the Moon?

14.   What is the name of the location on the moon where the Apollo 11 crew landed for the first time on July 21, 1969?

15.   The newspaper *Izvestia* is associated with which country?

16.   In which city is the International Court of Justice located?

17.   Name the Greek philosopher who wrote *The Republic*.

18.   What is the designation of the Head of State of Germany?

19.   How long is the Great Wall of China?

20. When is the U.N. Human Rights Day celebrated?

21. What is the tallest mountain in Africa?

22. Who was the first woman president of the U.N. General Assembly?

23. Where is the headquarters of the International Red Cross Society?

24. What does the abbreviation GNP stand for?

25. Who was the first man to reach the South Pole?

26. Who discovered the route to India via the Cape of Good Hope?

27. Who lives in the Elysee Palace?

28. Name the sculptor who created "The Thinker."

29. For what is Louis Braille famous?

30. Name the tree whose branch is a symbol of peace.

31. How did the month of January get its name?

The United Nations

The United Nations (U.N.) is headquartered in New York City, N.Y. The U.N. and its related bodies also maintain offices around the world.

The U.N. was established to maintain world peace. On June 26, 1945 a charter was signed by 50 nations and Poland to set up a body of nations dedicated to peace. The charter went into effect on October 24, 1945.

The current Secretary General of the U.N. is Koffi Annan of Ghana.

32. A sextant is used for what purpose?

33. Who was the youngest person to win the Nobel Prize?

34. Which European country is not a member of the United Nations?

35. What is the name of the currency used in Sweden?

36. Which two months are named after Roman emperors?

37. Which bird never makes its own nest?

38. Name one word which describes the art of making maps.

39. What name is given to low, horizontal clouds arranged in layers?

40. Give the full name of the famous comedian who starred in movies *City Lights* and *The Gold Rush*.

41. Claustrophobia is the fear of confined spaces. What is the fear of open spaces called?

42. If someone said he is a silviculturist, what is his profession?

43. Whom do the famous Swiss guards protect?

Symbols & You

Match the symbols on the left with the words on the right.

Your Answers:

A.

Exit

A. _____

B.

Recycle

B. _____

C.

Quite

C. _____

D.

Radioactive

D. _____

ANSWERS: **A.** *Quite* **B.** *Radioactive* **C.** *Recycle* **D.** *Exit*

44. From which plant are linseed oil and linen obtained?

45. Which of the Seven Wonders of the ancient world stood at Rhodes?

46. What does the name Dar-es-Salaam mean?

47. What is the name of the deepest known trench in the ocean?

48. What is the name of the Roman palace that is now the official residence of the President of Italy?

A Swiss Guard

49. Which country operates the airline carrier named Sabena?

50. Who painted "The Last Supper"?

51. Which Knight of the Round Table had eyes for the Queen?

52. What are the minimum and maximum numbers of possible solar eclipses in a given year?

53. Which was the first ship to circumnavigate the world?

54. What is the national flower of the Netherlands?

55. What was the nationality of the painter Francisco Jose de Lucientes y Goya?

56. What is goniometry?

FYI FYI FYI FYI

Do you know who paid the first income taxes?

The citizens of Florence, Italy were the first to pay income taxes. Under the rule of the famous Florentine family the Medicis, an income tax was instituted in 1451. At that time, the Florentines called it the "scala". In 1492, the "scala" was eventually abolished when the Medicis no longer the ruled the city.

57. Which two dog breeds were combined to make the Boxer?

58. What is the essential difference between rocket and jet fuel?

59. Which city did Jack the Ripper terrorize in 1888?

60. Where is the Acropolis?

Winged Horse
The symbol of poetry.

61. A winged horse in Greek mythology became the symbol of poetry. What was the horse's name?

62. Where are the Pillars of Hercules?

63. Where did the ukelele originate?

64. What type of animal is an ibex?

65. What is a puffin?

66. Who began a war with the abduction of Helen of Troy?

67. Where is the painting "Mona Lisa" permanently located?

68. What is the name of the volcano which erupted and buried Pompeii?

69. After whom is the month of March named?

70. To which country does Madeira belong?

71. What is La Scala and where is it located?

72. What is the literal meaning of the word "photography," which is derived from a Greek word?

73. A dulcimer is a musical instrument. How is it played?

74. What is the popular name of Mozart's last symphony?

75. Who was the Greek God of the Sun?

76. What do we call the leading female singer in an opera?

77. Which famous painter cut off his ear in a fit of depresion?

78. In which country was the piano invented?

79. Who composed "The Blue Danube?"

80. What is the name of the school of painting of which Cézanne was the chief advocate?

81. Who was the messenger of the Roman and Greek gods?

Uncle Sam
Mr. USA

82. If Uncle Sam symbolizes the United States, who symbolizes Great Britain?

83. Who was the Roman equivalent of the Greek goddess Athena?

84. Of the three gods forming the Hindu Trinity, who is the Protector?

85. The constellation Gemini (the Twins) portrays a pair of twins from Greek mythology. What are their names?

86. What famous literary family lived at Haworth Parsonage?

87. Where was Ludwig van Beethoven born and how many symphonies did he write?

88. Whose tomb is beneath the "Arc de Triomphe" in Paris?

89. Who was Anne Hathaway?

90. What is the title of respect applied to a Muslim who has memorized the Koran?

Arc de Triomphe located in Central Paris.

91. What kind of an animal is a goa?

92. Which country's national dance is the Highland Fling?

93. What is the name of King Arthur's sword?

94. The Riksdag is the parliament of which country?

95. Who invented the transistor?

96. To which family does the present British monarch belong?

97. Who invented the zipper?

98. Which famous explorer set sail with the ships *Conception, San Antonio, Santiago* and *Trinidad*?

99. English is the official language of one Central American country. Which country is it?

100. What were the middle names of Winston Churchill?

Sir Winston Churchill
(1874-1965)

Sir Winston Churchill was one of the greatest statesman of the world. In 1940, he was elected the British Prime Minister. Under his leadership, Britain successfully defended herself from Nazi Germany. According to Churchill's wishes, he was buried in Blandon churchyard rather than in Westminster Abbey in London after his death.

101. What is the family name of the famous composer Johannes Chrysostomus Wolfgangus Theophilus?

102. Which two South American countries have no maritime coast?

103. Which rare earth element is named after the character in Greek mythology who stole fire from heaven and gave it to man?

104. If you landed at Narita Airport, in which city have you arrived?

105. Which great man was tried at the Council at Worms in 1521?

106. Name the artist who painted "The Angelus".

107. The names of the days Thursday and Friday are derived from what?

108. What was the original name of the U.S. Presidential retreat Camp David in Maryland?

109. What Jordanian capital city was once called Philadelphia?

110. Who was the first Republican President?

111. What nation offered Albert Einstein its Presidential position in 1952?

112. What is the name of the Greek god of confusion?

113. What U.S. state was the first to secede from the Union?

114. Who is Agnes Gonxha Bojaxhin?

115. What color is Mr. Spock's *(Star Trek)* blood?

• *End of Trivia Questions* •

Master Painters
The Italians

Match the Master Painters on the left with their Paintings on the right

Your Answers: **A. ___   B. ___   C. ___   D. ___   E. ___   F. ___   G. ___**

A. Michelangelo

B. Domenico di Michelino

C. Aristotile da Sangallo

D. Pietro Perugino

E. Ambrogio Lorenzetti

F. Sandro Botticelli

G. Paolo Uccello

1. Allegory of Good Government

2. The Battle of Cascina

3. The Delphic Sibyl

4. The Hunt in the Forest

5. The Birth of Venus

6. The Archangel Raphael with Tobias

7. Dante Standing Before Florence

ANSWERS: A. 3   B. 7   C. 2   D. 6   E. 4   F. 1   G. 5

Word Quest
Political Figures

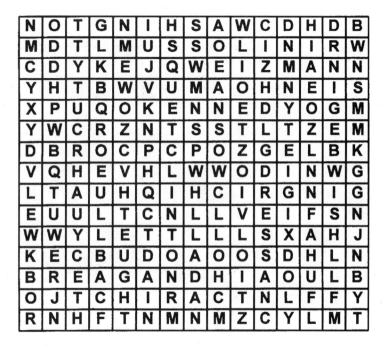

Search for the following politcal leaders:

Begin	Clinton	Lenin	Sadat
Bhutto	Dole	Mandela	Thatcher
Blair	Dubcek	Mao	Washington
Brandt	Gandhi	Nasser	Weizmann
Chirac	Gingrich	Reagan	Zedillo
Churchill	Kennedy	Roosevelt	
Clemenceau			

Cross Word Puzzle
General

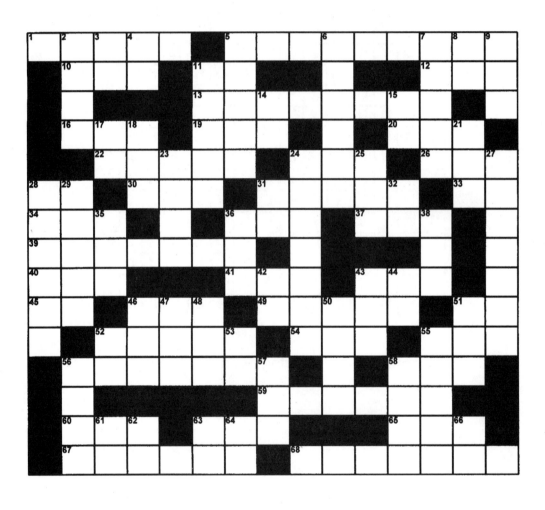

Across

1. speak
5. a food dish
10. an African fish
11. tone in diatonic scale
12. top executive
13. mishap
16. measure of print (pl)
19. eggs
20. however
22. largest artery
24. mesh
26. connection
28. connecting word
30. stocking (Fr)
31. stimulant
33. type tray
34. Apollo's son
36. continent (abbr)
37. Hebrew letter
39. most deafening
40. superlative
41. haw, as cattle
43. alder tree (scot)
45. right (abbr)
46. Finn in Ingria
49. dwarf
51. them (singular)
52. more sheltered
54. intestines
55. three (ital)
56. comprise
58. Scottish oak
59. unbroken
60. Aspen ____ Resort
63. Dutch dry measure
65. stitchbird
67. compositions
68. preparatory school

Down

2. exhaust
3. Norse god of war
4. Ethyleneoxide
5. chocolate
6. sooner than expected
7. eight musicians
8. article (fr)
9. government agency (acr)
11. rush about
14. engineering degree
15. borders Canada
17. goddess of fertility
18. lament
21. link
23. frenzy
24. wordage
25. fragment
27. imitate
28. Houston team
29. perch
31. you (sp)
32. most populous state
35. pecan, cashew
36. ordinal number suffix
38. moving vehicle
42. officer of guard (abbr)
43. Norwegian territory
44. football position (acr)
46. cargo vehicle
47. frequently
48. social affair
50. remove
51. irritate
52. consequently
53. borders Connecticut
55. one tenth
56. bag
57. bite
58. hydrochloric _____
61. Kansas
62. King Gradlon's capital
63. blue grass state
64. mouth
66. swimming event

Cross Word Puzzle
Noted Business Leaders

Across

1. Chicago Bulls Owner
3. American Airlines' CEO
7. Walt Disney's CEO
8. Coca Cola's CEO
9. FedEx's CEO
10. Microsoft's CEO
11. Viacom Inc.'s CEO
13. Dallas Cowboys Owner
14. Westinghouse's CEO
15. TCI Cable's CEO

Down

2. New York Times' CEO
4. Founder of Kodak
5. Washinton Post's CEO
6. Reebok's CEO
12. Founder of CNN
13. Founder of Apple Computer

FYI   FYI   FYI   FYI

*Did you know that the Disney Studio named the seven dwarfs and **not** the Brothers Grimm?*

The names of the seven dwarfs who appeared in Disney's 1937 production *Snow White and the Seven Dwarfs* were: Bashful, Doc, Dopey, Grumpy, Happy, Sleepy and Sneezy.

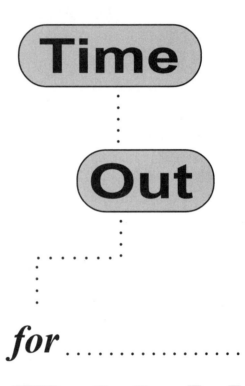

for

F U N

Incredible
Facts
for
the
Curious Mind

More Incredible but True Facts... Part 1

Bank robber John Dillinger was a former professional baseball player.

Mickey Mouse is known as Topolino in Italy.

One in two billion people will live to be 115 years or older.

Every Swiss citizen is required by law to have a bomb shelter or access to a bomb shelter.

- The cheetah is the only cat in the world that cannot retract its claws.

- An average sixty minute audio cassette tape is 562.5 feet in length.

- The cable cars of San Francisco are the only mobile national monuments.

- West Virginia is the only state in the continental United States without a natural lake.

- Since the beginning of modern Olympics in 1896, Greece and Australia are the only nations to have participated in every Olympiad.

- Montpelier, Vermont is the only state capital without a McDonalds.

- Two-thirds of the cobalt produced in the world is mined in Zaire, Africa.

- The three leading cork producing countries in the world are Spain, Portugal and Algeria.

- The first video played on MTV Europe was Dire Straits' "Money for

Nothing."

- Cats cannot move their jaws sideways.

- An average human produces a quart of saliva each day.

- The great Egyptian Phaoroh Ramses II fathered over 160 children.

- A pregnant goldfish is called a twit.

- A dime has 118 ridges around its edge.

- New Jersey is home to a spoon museum featuring more than 5000 spoons from every state and country.

- Carson City, Nevada celebrates Halloween on October 30th every year.

- Leonardo da Vinci spend nearly twelve years painting Mona Lisa's lips.

- Lightning strikes the Earth approximately two hundred times a second.

- Ketchup was once used as a medicine in the United States.

- The Earth experiences approximately 50,000 earthquakes a year.

- Hair grows at a rate of one-hundredth of an inch per day.

- Daniel Webster originated the custom of standing when the national anthem is played.

- Bird droppings are the primary export commodity of the western Pacific island nation of Nauru.

- Alexander the Great had epilepsy.

- The language Malayalam, spoken in southern India, is the only language which is a palindrome.

- Panama hats come from Ecuador not Panama.

- A full moon always rises at sunset.

- An elephant may be pregnant for as long as 24 months.

- An average regulation golf ball has 336 dimples on it.

- "Video Killed the Radio Star" was the very first video played on MTV.

- A human needs an average of 43 muscles inorder to frown.

- An average human body contains enough water to fill a 10 gallon tank.

- 9,500,000,000 minutes of telephone calls are logged during an average business day in the United States.

- In a 1990 study of the windiest cities in the US, Chicago (The Windy City) was ranked a lowly 21.

- The French consume nearly 200 million frogs a year.

All About Food
Where do they come from?

The World's Largest Producer of ...

Grapes • Italy	**Coconut** • Indonesia	**Corn** • U.S.
Apple • U.S.	**Pear** • China	**Rice** • China
Peach • Italy	**Banana** • India	**Potato** • Russia
Orange • Brazil	**Mango** • India	**Wheat** • China
Pineapple • Thailand	**Strawberry** • U.S.	**Sugar Cane** • Brazil

All About Food
What Supermarkets Do They End Up In?

Largest U.S. Supermarkets

The Kroger Company

Safeway

American Stores

Winn-Dixie

The Great Atlantic and Pacific Tea Company

Albertson's

Food Lion

Publix

The Vons Companies

Pathmark Supermarkets

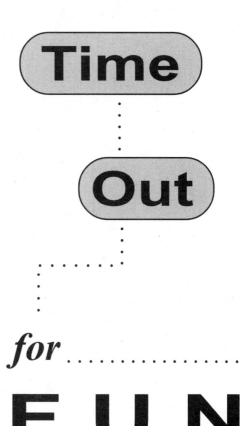

Time

Out

for

F U N

Incredible
Facts
for
the
Curious Mind

*More Incredible **but** True Facts... Part 2*

An estimated 200 million M&Ms are sold in the U.S. everyday.

Cleopatra used pomegranate seeds as lipstick.

The smallest post office is located in Ochopee, Florida.

Jesus Christ died at the age of 33.

Elizabeth I of England suffered from anthophobia (fear of roses).

- The technical term "Unix" is a registered trademark of AT&T.

- The words "race car" is a palindrome.

- The glue on Israeli postage stamps is a certified kosher product.

- New York City's Battery Park City was created from the large quantity of soil that was dug up to create the foundation of the World Trade Center.

- Hummingbirds are the only birds that can fly backwards.

- Wilma Flintstone's maiden name was Wilma Slaghoopal.

- Unlike records which are read from the outside edge to the inside edge, compact discs are read from the inside out.

- In the Disney classic "Fantasia," the sorcerer's name is Yensid (Disney spelled backwards).

- The world's largest cave opening, Cathedral Caverns, is located near Grant, Alabama.

- All swans in England are the property of the Queen.

- The TV show "Leave it to Beaver" and the Russian satellite Sputnik were launched on the same date – October 4, 1957.

- The shortest intercontinental commercial flight in the world is between Gibraltar to Tangier (Morocco, Africa).

- The longest non-stop commercial flight is from New York City to Johannesburg, South Africa.

- Barbie's full name is Barbra Millicent Roberts.

- Great Britain is the only country in the world that does not print its name on its stamps.

- The silhouette on the NBA logo is that of Jerry West, a former Los Angeles Lakers great.

- There are more than 2,000 varieties of bats and most of them eat insects.

- One fifth of the oxygen we inhale is utilized by brain cells.

- The famous Leonardo da Vinci painting "Mona Lisa" was first bought by Francis I, King of France, who used it to decorate one of his many bathrooms.

- Horses lack collar bones.

- Saudi Arabia imports sand from Scotland and camels from North Africa.

- Milk is heavier than cream.

- There is no income tax in the Middle Eastern nations of Bahrain, Kuwait and Qatar.

- The sun weighs 330,000 times as much as the Earth.

- A full moon is nine times brighter than a half moon.

- Croatia was the first country to recognize the United States in 1776.

- On average, each human being shares his or her birthday with 10 million other people.

- Zebras have white stripes not black ones.

- The luckiest number in Italy is 13.

- The Earth is approximately 4600 million years old.

- The twenty six letters of the English language alphabet can be recombined 620,448,401,733,239,439,369,000 times.

- An average person drinks about 16,000 gallons of water during his or her lifetime.

- The Swiss flag is perfectly square in shape.

- There are six grams of gold in an Olympic Gold Medal.

- An average bank teller misplaces about $250 a year.

- Approximately 130 million cups of coffee are consumed in the United States everyday.

All About Airports
On Top of the World

Five Busiest Airports	
1. O'Hare International	Chicago
2. Hartsfield Interntl.	Atlanta
3. Dallas/Ft. Worth Intl.	Dallas/Ft. Worth
4. Heathrow Airport	London
5. Los Angeles Intl.	Los Angeles

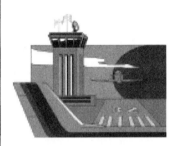

Top Duty-Free Airports	
1. Honolulu Airport	Hawaii
2. Hong Kong Airport	Hong Kong
3. Heathrow Airport	London
4. Amsterdam Schiphol	The Netherlands
5. Charles de Gaulle	Paris

World's Largest Corporations
The Top Earners

Mitsubishi (Japan)

Mitsui (Japan)

Itochu (Japan)

Sumitomo (Japan)

General Motors (U.S.)

Marubeni (Japan)

Ford Motor Company (U.S.)

Exxon (U.S.)

Nissho Iwai (Japan)

Royal Dutch-Shell Group (U.K./Holland)

Toyota Motor (Japan)

Wal-Mart (U.S.)

Hitachi (Japan)

Nippon Life Insurance (Japan)

Matsushita Electric (Japan)

Tomen (Japan)

General Electric (U.S.)

Daimler-Benz (Germany)

IBM (U.S.)

Mobil (U.S.)

Nissan Motor (U.S.)

Nichimen (Japan)

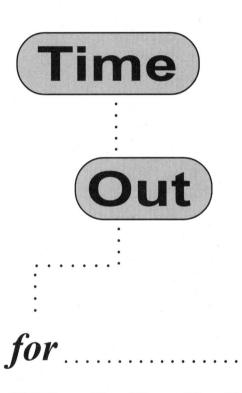

Incredible
Facts
for
the
Curious Mind

More Incredible but True Facts… Part 3

First Time Ever

■ **First Inventions in Medicine**

Aspirin – or *acetylsalicylic acid* was first synthesized by Charles Gerhardt at the University of Montpellier (France) in 1853.

Incubator – was invented by Budin (French) in 1880.

Virus – was discovered by Ivanovsky (Russian) in 1892.

Anti-flu vaccine – was discovered by Jonas Salk (American) in 1937.

Microscope – was invented by J. Jansen and his son Zacharias (Dutch) during the 16th century.

Pacemaker – was invented by Ake Senning (Swede) in 1958.

Vitamin C – was first isolated by Gyorgyi (Hungarian) in 1928.

Interferon – was discovered by Isaacs (English) and Lindenmann (Swiss) in 1957.

Blood circulation – was first defined by William Harvey (English) in 1628.

■ **First Inventions in Mathematics**

Arithmetic – originated some time during the 6th century B.C.

Logarithms – was invented by John Napier (Scottish) in 1614.

Probability Theory – was established by Christian Huygens (Dutch) in 1656.

Statistics – was introduced by Gottfried Achenwall (German) in 1748.

Elliptical Geometry – was founded by Bernhard Riemann (German) in 1854.

Calculus – was invented by Sir Isaac Newton (English) in 1665.

■ **First Inventions in Transportation**

Jumbo Jet (Boeing 747) – made its first flight on February 9, 1969.

Concorde – made its first flight on March 12, 1969.

Glider – was invented by Sir George Cayley (English) in 1809.

Subway – was first operated in London, England in 1863.

Electric Locomotive – was first used on the Baltimore-Ohio train line (U.S.) in 1895.

Wheel – has been part of the human civilization since 3500 B.C.

Lighthouse – was first built by King Ptolemy II in Egypt in 285 B.C.

Oil Tanker - was first built in Germany in 1886.

■ **First Inventions in Food Industry**

Chocolate Bar – was first manufactured by Francois-Louis Cailler (Swiss) in 1819.

Margarine – was invented by Hippolyte Mege-Mouries (French) in 1869.

Saccharin – was discovered by Constantin Fahlberg (American) in 1879.

Eskimo Pie (Ice Cream) – was invented by C. Nelson (American) in 1922.

Coca-Cola – was invented by a pharmacist named John Pemberton in Atlanta, Georgia in 1886.

Champagne – was first produced by Dom Pierre Perignon, a monk and physician, of France in 1688.

■ **First Inventions in Publishing**

Papyrus – was invented by the Egyptians around 1800 B.C.

Ink – was invented in China in 2500 B.C.

Pencil – was invented after the discovery of graphite in the 16th century.

Classified Ads – were first published by Thomas Newcome (English) in 1657.

Carbon Paper – was invented by R. Wedgewood (English) in 1806.

Typewriter – was invented by Xavier Progin (French) in Marseilles in 1833.

- **First Inventions in Music**

Modern Guitar – was developed by A. de Torres (Spanish) in 1850.

Clarinet – was invented by J. Denner (German) in 1670.

Jazz – was originated around 1885 in New Orleans, Louisiana.

Magnetic recording tape – was first made by Fritz Pfleumer in 1928.

Audio cassette – was first made by Philips of the Netherlands in 1963.

Saxophone – was invented by Adolphe Sax (Belgian) in 1846.

- **First Inventions in Home Appliances**

Thermos – was invented by a Scottish physicist named Sir James Dewar in 1906.

Microwave oven – was deviced by Percy Le Baron Spencer (American) and the Raytheon company in 1947.

Pressure cooker – was invented by Hautuer (French) in 1927.

Toasters – were first manufactured by the General Electric Company (U.S.) in 1909.

A Quick Stroll Through
The 20th Century

1900 William McKinley is re-elected President of the U.S.

Renoir paints *"Nude in the Sun"*.

Nietzsche dies.

Radon, an element, is discovered.

1904 Theodore Roosevelt elected President of the U.S.

Henry James's *"The Golden Bowl"* is published.

Rolls Royce company is established.

The painter Salvatore Dali is born in Spain.

1910 NAACP is founded.

The Manhattan Bridge, which spans New York City's East River, opens to the public.

1914 World War I starts in Europe.

Panama Canal is opened in Central America.

Tennessee Williams is born.

Edgar Burroughs introduces the fictional character Tarzan.

1920   The League of Nations formed.

Walther Nernst wins the Noble Prize for Chemistry.

First U.S. radio station is opened in Pittsburgh, Pennsylvania.

19th Amendment of the U.S. Constitution awards women the right to vote.

Babe Ruth traded by the Boston Red Sox to the New York Yankees.

1926   The House of Saud is established by Ibn Saud in Saudi Arabia.

Henry Houdini dies.

The world's first 16 mm film is produced.

Queen Elizabeth II (the current Queen of England) is born.

1929   The U.S. Stock exchange collapses.

Leon Trotsky expelled from Russia.

Vitamin K is discovered.

Virginia Woolf's *"A Room of One's Own"* is published.

1932   The British government declares India's Congress illegal.

Both the positron and the neutron are discovered by scientists.

Charles Lindbergh's baby is kidnapped from his home in New Jersey.

Amelia Earhart becomes the first woman to fly solo across the Atlantic.

1936   King Edward VIII abdicates the throne of England.

Life magazine is published for the first time.

Trotsky settles in Mexico.

Jesse Owens wins four gold medals at the Berlin Olympics.

1939   Sigmund Freud dies.

Civil War ends in Spain.

World War II begins when England and France declare war on Germany on September 3rd.

1944   D-Day landings takes place in Normandy, France on June 6.

Franklin D. Roosevelt elected to a fourth term as President of the United States.

Rommel commits suicide.

1948

Babe Ruth dies.

Mahatma Gandhi is assassinated in India.

Israel is founded.

The World Council of Churches is formed.

T. S. Eliot awarded the Noble Prize in Literature.

1953

Dag Hammarskjöld of Sweden elected Secretary General of the United Nations.

Hillary and Tenzing conquer Mt. Everest.

Convicted spies Rosenbergs are executed in the United States.

1958

Van Allen radiation belt detected around the Earth.

Charles de Gaulle elected President of France.

The European Community Market is formed.

Stereo sound invented.

Alaska becomes the 49th U.S. state.

Boris Pasternak awarded the Noble Prize for Literature.

1962

Adolf Eichmann is hanged.

U Thant of Burma elected Secretary General of the U.N.

Former First Lady Eleanor Roosevelt dies.

Uganda becomes an independent nation.

1965

Winston Churchill, a former Prime Minister of England, dies.

Malcolm X assassinated in New York City.

Medicare is established in the U.S.

Edward R. Murrow, a famous journalist, dies.

Charles de Gaulle is re-elected President of France.

Author T. S. Eliot dies.

Singapore admitted to the U.N.

Martin Luther King, Jr. organizes a civil rights march from Selma to Montgomery, Alabama.

1967

President Johnson appoints noted jurist Thurgood Marshall to the U.S. Supreme Court.

The world's first human heart transplant is performed in South Africa.

Six-Day War starts between Israel and Arab nations.

1969   U.S. astronauts land on the moon on July 24th.

Richard Nixon inaugurated President of the U.S.

Ho Chi Minh dies in Vietnam.

Woodstock Music Festival takes place in Bethel, N.Y.

Yasir Arafat elected Chairman of the Executive Committee of the PLO.

1971   Switzerland grants women the right to vote.

India and Pakistan go to war in Asia.

Cigarette advertisements banned on U.S. television.

The 26th Amendment to the Constitution granting 18 year olds the right to vote, is ratified in the U.S.

1977   More than 500 passengers die when a KLM Boeing 747 and a Pan American Boeing 747 collide in Tenerife, Spain.

Martial law is instituted in Pakistan.

New York Yankees win the World Series.

Leonid Brezhnev becomes President of the Soviet Union.

Indira Gandhi resigns as Prime Minister of India.

Steven Biko dies in South Africa.

1980

The U.S. and Iran break off diplomatic ties.

Mount St. Helens volcano erupts in the U.S. Pacific Northwest.

The wreck of the Titanic is discovered in the North Atlantic Ocean.

Smallpox is eradicated worldwide.

1984

Ray Kroc, the founder of McDonald's, dies.

Bishop Desmond Tutu of South Africa is awarded the Noble Peace Prize.

Re-elected Indian Prime Minister Indira Gandhi is assassinated.

President Reagan re-elected President of the U.S.

Ansel Adams, a noted American photographer, dies.

A toxic gas leak in Bhopal, India kills 2,500 people.

The U.S. and the Vatican establish a diplomatic relationship.

Donald Duck celebrates his 50th birthday.

1988

Russian troops begin their withdrawl from Afghanistan.

Naguib Mahfouz (Egypt) becomes the first African writer to win the Noble Prize for Literature.

Seoul, South Korea hosts the Summer Olympics.

1990 General Manuel Noriega of Panama surrenders to U.S. troops.

Portrait of Dr. Gachet by Van Gogh sells for $82.5 million.

Mikhail Gorbachev (Russia) wins the Noble Peace Prize.

West Germany wins Soccer's World Cup.

Nelson Mandela is freed from jail.

Mary Robinson becomes the first female Prime Minister of Ireland.

1992 Barcelona, Spain hosts the Summer Olympics.

William Jefferson Clinton elected President of the U.S.

Talk show host Johnny Carson bids farewell to *The Tonight Show.*

Hurricane Andrew hits Florida killing 61 people.

1994 Nelson Mandela elected President of South Africa.

The Unites States host Soccer's World Cup.

Pop star Michael Jackson marries Lisa Marie Presley.

Two million refugees from Rwanda escape to neighboring countries to avoid massacre.

The 50th anniversary of D-Day celebrated in France.

Former football great O. J. Simpson is accused of killing Nicole Brown Simpson and Ronald Goldman.

1997 Tony Blair elected Prime Minister of England.

A severe earthquake kills thousands in Iran.

Mobutu Sese Seko's long reign in Zaire comes to an end.

Scientists in England announce the successful cloning of sheep.

The Green Bay Packers win the Super Bowl.

The 20th Century
The Age of Technology

The Map Game

Time

Out

for ....

F U N

Where Are We?

Find the following European countries: Finland, France, Great Britain, Greece, Germany, Italy, Norway, Spain, Switzerland and the Netherlands

Your Answers:

A. _____

B. _____

C. _____

D. _____

E. _____

F. _____

G. _____

H. _____

I. _____

J. _____

North Sea

Atlantic Ocean

Mediterranean Sea

D   E   C   F   G   B   H   I   A   J

ANSWERS: **A.** *Spain* **B.** *France* **C.** *Great Britain* **D.** *Norway* **E.** *Finland* **F.** *The Netherlands* **G.** *Germany* **H.** *Switzerland* **I.** *Italy* **J.** *Greece*

Where Are We?

Find the following Asian countries: Borneo, Burma, China, India, Iran, Mongolia and Saudi Arabia

Your Answers:

A. _____

B. _____

C. _____

D. _____

E. _____

F. _____

G. _____

ANSWERS: **A.** *Saudi Arabia* **B.** *Iran* **C.** *India* **D.** *Mongolia* **E.** *China*
F. *Burma* **G.** *Borneo*

Where Are We?

Find the following American states: California, Florida, Georgia, Illinois, Louisiana, Nebraska, New York, Ohio, Texas and Washington

Your Answers:

A. _____

B. _____

C. _____

D. _____

E. _____

F. _____

G. _____

H. _____

I. _____

J. _____

ANSWERS: **A.** *Washington* **B.** *California* **C.** *Nebraska* **D.** *Illinois* **E.** *Ohio*
F. *New York* **G.** *Texas* **H.** *Louisiana* **I.** *Georgia* **J.** *Florida*

The Matching Game

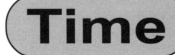 Time

Out

for . . . .

F U N

American Literature

Match the books on the left with the authors on the right.

		Your Answers:
A. Sons and Lovers	F. Scott Fitzgerald	**A.** _____
B. Free Fall	John Steinbeck	**B.** _____
C. Babbitt	Ernest Hemingway	**C.** _____
D. The Living Reed	William Golding	**D.** _____
E. A Moveable Feast	William Styron	**E.** _____
F. This Side of Paradise	D. H. Lawrence	**F.** _____
G. The Winter of Our Discontent	Sinclair Lewis	**G.** _____
H. Sophie's Choice	Pearl S. Buck	**H.** _____

Answers: A: Lawrence B. Golding C. Lewis D. Buck E. Hemingway F. Fitzgerald G. Steinbeck H. Styron

Money, Money, Money

Match the currencies on the left with the countries on the right.

		Your Answers:
A. Guilder	Guatemala	**A.** ———
B. Franc	Italy	**B.** ———
C. Yen	Thailand	**C.** ———
D. Baht	Sweden	**D.** ———
E. Quetzal	Nicaragua	**E.** ———
F. Lira	Japan	**F.** ———
G. Cordoba	France	**G.** ———
H. Krona	The Netherlands	**H.** ———

Answers:
A: The Netherlands   B. France   C. Japan   D. Thailand   E. Guatemala   F. Italy   G. Nicaragua   H. Sweden

State Nicknames

Match the nicknames on the left with the states on the right.

		Your Answers:
A. Aloha State	New Mexico	**A.** _____
B. Empire State	California	**B.** _____
C. Land of Enchantment	Indiana	**C.** _____
D. Grand Canyon State	South Carolina	**D.** _____
E. Golden State	Hawaii	**E.** _____
F. Hoosier State	Wyoming	**F.** _____
G. Palmetto State	Arizona	**G.** _____
H. Equality State	New York	**H.** _____

Answers: A: Hawaii B. New York C. New Mexico D. Arizona E. California F. Indiana G. South Carolina H. Wyoming

Screen Names of Entertainers

Match the screen names on the left with the original names on the right.

A. Julie Andrews	Gordon Summer	**Your Answers:**
		A. _____
B. Tom Cruise	Larry Zeigler	
		B. _____
C. Whoopi Goldberg	David Atkins	
		C. _____
D. Larry King	Julia Wells	
		D. _____
E. Soupy Sales	Annie Mae Bullock	
		E. _____
F. Sinbad	Thomas Mapother	
		F. _____
G. Sting	Caryn Johnson	
		G. _____
H. Tina Turner	Milton Hines	
		H. _____

Answers: A: Wells B. Mapother C. Johnson D. Zeigler E. Hines F. Atkins G. Sumner H. Bullock

Brand Names

Match the consumer products on the left with their manufacturers on the right.

		Your Answers:
A. Ben-Gay	Quaker Oats	A. _____
B. Cheez Whiz	Johnson & Johnson	B. _____
C. Gatorade	3M	C. _____
D. Hamburger Helper	Pfizer	D. _____
E. Life Savers candy	Dow Chemical	E. _____
F. Post-It stickers	Philip Morris	F. _____
G. Tylenol	General Mills	G. _____
H. Ziploc storage bags	RJR Nabisco	H. _____

Answers: A: Pfizer B. Philip Morris C. Quaker Oats D. General Mills E. RJR Nabisco F. 3M G. Johnson & Johnson H. Dow Chemical

International Soccer

Match the teams on the left with their home cities on the right.

			Your Answers:
A. Ajax	London, England		**A.** _____
B. Sampdoria	Rio de Janeiro, Brazil		**B.** _____
C. Mohun Bagan	East Rutherford, New Jersey, U.S.		**C.** _____
D. Flamingo	Buenos Aires, Argentina		**D.** _____
E. Metrostars	Nagoya, Japan		**E.** _____
F. Boca Juniors	Calcutta, India		**F.** _____
G. Chelsea	Genoa, Italy		**G.** _____
H. Grampus Eight	Amsterdam, The Netherlands		**H.** _____

Answers: A: Amsterdam B. Genoa C. Calcutta D. Rio de Janeiro E. East Rutherford F. Buenos Aires
G. London H. Nagoya

Inventors

Match the inventions on the left with their inventors on the right.

		Your Answers:
A. Telephone	Pierre Verdan	**A.** _____
B. Phonograph	Theodore Maiman	**B.** _____
C. Fountain Pen	Ralph Schneider	**C.** _____
D. Vacuum Cleaner	Alexander G. Bell	**D.** _____
E. Credit Card	C. Gould	**E.** _____
F. Food Processor	Thomas Edison	**F.** _____
G. Stapler	Hubert Booth	**G.** _____
H. Laser	Lewis Waterman	**H.** _____

Answers: A: Bell B. Edison C. Waterman D. Booth E. Schneider F. Verdan
G. Gould H. Maiman

Geography

Answers

Geography Answers

1. The Pacific Ocean and it was named by Ferdinand Magellan. Excluding adjacent seas, the Pacific Ocean represents 45.8% of the worlds ocean. The average depth of the Pacific Ocean is 4200 meters.

2. Accra

3. The Netherlands

4. Java Trench – 23175 feet (7725 meters) deep

5. Oslo

6. Palk Strait

7. The Sahara

Top Five Deep Sea Trenches	
1. Mariana	Pacific Ocean
2. Tonga	Pacific Ocean
3. Philippine	Pacific Ocean
4. Kermadec	Pacific Ocean
5. Bonin	Pacific Ocean

Nearly an eighth of the world's land surface, it is arid with an annual rainfall of less than 25 cm. The Sahara stretchs approximately 3220 miles in an East to West direction. From North to South, the desert stretchs between 800 to 1400 miles.

Five Largest Deserts	
1. Sahara	North Africa
2. Australian	Australia
3. Arabian	Asia
4. Gobi	China-Mongolia
5. Kalahari	Africa

8.   Hamburg

9.   Thailand

10.   The Amazon
The Amazon is is approximately 4025 miles long. It runs from its source on Mount Huagra, north of Guillama, Peru to the mouth of the Rio do Para Channel, Brazil in the South Atlantic. It is navigable for its entire length within Brazil and discharges more water than any river on Earth.

11.   Europe

12.   The River Tiber

It is 250 miles long and flows through Rome into the Mediterranean Sea.

13.   South Korea

South Korea

Independence Day: August 15

Location: South Korea is located in the Korean peninsula in Northeast Asia.

Government Type: Republic

Population: 45 million

Three largest cities: Seoul (Capital), Pusan and Taegi.

Currency: Won

14.   Lima

15.   Lake Superior

16.   At the southern tip of South America.

17.   Abel Janszoon Tasman, a Dutchman, in 1642.

18. Africa

19. Four minutes.
     When travelling from East to West, a clock would have to be
     would 4 minutes for every degree of longitude travelled.

20. Venice

21. The delta created by River Ganges and Brahmaputra. The 47,000
     square mile delta spans across parts of India and Bangladesh.

22. Lake Baikal located in Central Siberia.

23. Tartar Straits between Sakhalin Island and mainland Russia.

24. USA.
     Snake river rises in Wyoming and flows into Idaho. It is 940 miles

long.

25. Wellington. The capital was named after a British Prime Minister and soldier.

26. Gulf of Mexico
The gulf has a shoreline of 3119 miles from Cape Sable, Florida to Cabo Catoche, Mexico.

27. The Arabian Peninsula.
It is approximately 2 million square mile in area.

28. Isobars are lines on a map that joins places/regions that have the same atmospheric pressure.

29. The River Ob in Russia.
The river is nearly as long as the Mississipi. River Ob is joined by the Irtysh, its main tributary, to comprise Russia's largest river system of nearly 3500 miles.

30. Winchester

31. River Darling

32. Lake Michigan
Lakes Superior, Erie, Huron, and Ontario are shared by both US and Canada.

33. Sweden

34.   Berlin

35.   The Victoria Falls is located in the Upper **Zambezi River**. It is 1 mile wide and have a drop of approximately 128 meters. The thick mist and the loud roar of the falling water can be seen and heard from over 10 miles away. Discovered by David Livingstone, it was named after Queen Victoria of England.

36.   Ferdinand de Lesseps

37.   Rome

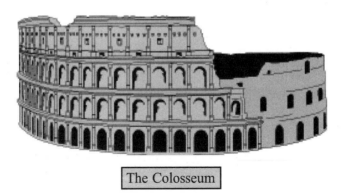

The Colosseum

38.   France and Spain

39.   Damascus, the capital of Syria.

40.   Le Havre

41. Egypt and Saudi Arabia

42. The Red Sea

43. Danube and Volga

44. France

45. Cairo, the capital of Egypt.
Cairo is also known as El Kahirah (the Victorious). The city is situated on the Nile and was founded in 969 A.D.

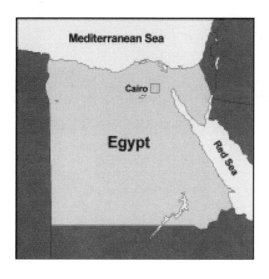

Egypt

Independence Day: February 28

Location: Egypt is located in the Northeastern section of Africa.

Government Type: Republic

Population: 61 million

Three largest cities: Cairo, Alexandria and Giza.

Currency: Egyptian pound

46. New Zealand

47. The United States and Canada

Where Are We?

Find the following African countries: Algeria, Egypt, Ethiopia, Madagascar, Mali, Namibia, South Africa, and Zaire

Your Answers:

A. _____

B. _____

C. _____

D. _____

E. _____

F. _____

G. _____

H. _____

Atlantic Ocean

Indian Ocean

ANSWERS: **A.** *Algeria* **B.** *Mali* **C.** *Egypt* **D.** *Ethiopia* **E.** *Zaire* **F.** *Namibia* **G.** *South Africa* **H.** *Madagascar*

48. Ghana (Africa)

49. Tunisia

50. Cape Town, South Africa

51. Athens. Its port is located in Piraeus.

52. Sumatra in Indian Ocean.

53. Scandinavian Peninsula

54. The Jawahar Pass

55. Honshu

56. The Kiel Canal

57. Mt. Kosciusko in New South Wales

58. Greece

59. Nyasaland

60. Mexico

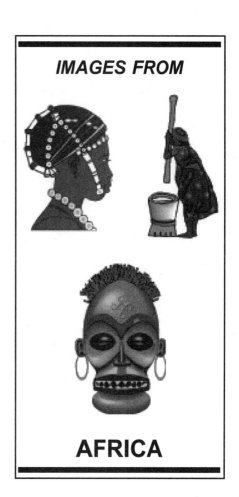

IMAGES FROM

AFRICA

61.   Mediterranean Sea. Balearic Islands belong to Spain.

Five Tallest Mountains	
1. Mt. Everest	Nepal
2. K2 (Godwin-Austen)	India-China
3. Kanchenjunga	Nepal
4. Lhotse	Nepal
5. Makalu	Nepal-Tibet

62.   K2. It was first conquered on July 31, 1754.

63.   Israel and Syria

64.   Belgium. Luxembourgh and the Netherlands

65.   Pampas

66.   Zambia

67.   Calabria.
The three provinces are Catanzaro, Cosenza and Reggio

68.   Tanzania

69. Ecuador

70. In Mali, West Africa

71. The United Kingdom

72. Ruanda
Nile's source was discovered by
John Hanning Speke in 1858.

The famous Opera House at the
Sydney Harbor in Australia.

73. Yes, Australia

74. River Rhine

75. The Cotswold Hills

76. River Nile

77. Approximately following the 180 meridian.

78. River Mississippi
The ten states are Arkansas, Illinois, Iowa, Kentucky, Louisiana,
Minnesota, Mississippi, Missouri, Tennessee, and Wisconsin.

79. Hong Kong

80. The Sirocco

81. Kra Isthmus links Burma and Thailand with Malaysia

82. The photosphere is the visible surface of the sun which can be seen as a bright disc from the Earth.

83. Pluto

84. Off the southern most tip of South America.

The first artificial satellite launched in space was *Sputnik I* (Russia).

85. Lesotho

86. River Amazon in South America

87. Kariba Dam

88. Isle of Wight

89. 1:109
     The approximate diameters of the Earth is 7971 miles and the sun is 868750 miles.

90. Mercury, Pluto and Venus
     The Earth has one, Mars has two, Jupitar has fourteen, Saturn has nine, Uranus has five and Neptune has two moons.

91. River Jordan

92. Michigan
It borders all Great Lakes except Lake Ontario.

93. La Manche

94. About 71% of the Earth's surface

95. The upper layer is called sial or sal.

96. Khamsin

97. Australia

98. Dolomite

99. French Guiana

100. Iraq

101. St. George's

102. Uganda, Kenya and Somalia

103. The eastern coast of India

104. Male (pronounced as Maali)

105. Mexico City

Cross Word Puzzle
World Cities 1 – Answer

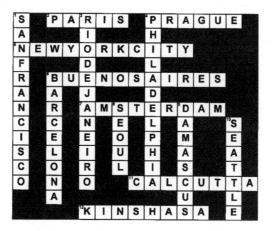

Cross Word Puzzle
World Cities 2 – Answer

History

Answers

World History Answers

1.   1690, by the British

2.   April 5th, 1968

3.   Alexandria

4.   The founder of modern Turkey. He proclaimed Turkey a republic in 1923. Ataturk became the first President of the country and served from 1923 to 1938. His birth name was Mustafa Kemal Pasha.

5.   August 6th, 1945

6.   Martin Luther (1483-1546)

7.   Dr. Sun yat Sen

8. Versailles Palace

9. 18th century

10. Nero

FYI   FYI   FYI   FYI

Who designed the American flag?

The American flag was designed by Francis Hopkinson, a naval flag designer.

11. Shah Jafar

12. Cicero

13. Marathon

14.　The Jain religion

15.　Constantine

16.　1786, under the reign of Louis XVII

17.　The Treaty of Versailles, signed June 28th, 1919.

18.　Italian

19.　General Francisco Franco

Longest Reigning Monarchs	
1. Louis XIV	France (72 years)
2. John II	Liechtenstein (71 Years)
3. Franz-Josef	Austria-Hungary (67 years)
4. Victoria	U.K. (59 years)
5. Hirohito	Japan (62 years)

20.　King Louis XIV of France. He reigned for 72 years.

21.　Temujin-Kurultai. The council of Mongol Khans gave him the title Genghis Khan, which means the greatest of rulers.

22.　The Queen of Sheba

23.　The Eagle

24.　Winston Churchill (UK), Harry Truman (US) and Joseph Stalin (Russia)

25. October 26th, 1971

26. Six

27. Herbert Henry Asquith

28. 1603, when James VI of Scotland succeeded Elizabeth I and thereby also became King James I of England.

29. The Japanese attack on Pearl Harbor.

30. Anwar Sadat

31. Admiral K. Doenitz

32. Henry VI was 9 months old when he became the King.

33. The Santa Maria.
    Together with two other small ships, the Pinta and the Nina, the Santa Maria set sail from Palos, Spain on August 3rd, 1492, on a voyage of discovery. The Santa Maria was wrecked on the north coast of Hispaniola on Christmas Eve, 1492.

34. In Russia.
    Golda Meir was born as Golda Mobovitz in Kiev, Russia. Her family immigrated to Milwaukee, USA in 1906.

35. The Alpingi of Iceland established in 930 A.D.

36. The Bourbons (1589-1848)

37. In Babylon in the year 232 B.C.

38. King William I
The Tower of London is an ancient fortress and royal residence located on the north bank of River Thames in London. For centuries, illustrious prisoners were also housed at the Tower.

39. At Pharsalus, Greece in 48 B.C.

40. Hernando Cortes.
Cortes was born in 1485. He crushed the Aztecs in Mexico with an expeditionary force that initially consisted of less than 600 Spaniards, a few natives, and 15 horses.

41. China

42. 1869

43. King Charles II

44. Romulus Augustus

45. Abyssinia

46. For four days.
More than 13,000 homes and 400 streets were destroyed by the

fire.

47. Winston Churchill.
In 1946, Churchill used the term "Iron Curtain"
todescribe the line of demarcation between Western Europe and
the Russian zone of influence.

48.   Admiral Lord Nelson

49.   The Punic Wars

50.   Lumbini, located at the Nepalese foot
hills near the Nepal-India border.

51.   "Dr. Livingstone, I presume!"

52.   The Spanish naval expedition of 1588
against England.

53.   570 A.D.

54.   The flag of Denmark dating from 1219.

Denmark
National Holiday: Queen's Birthday
Location: Northwestern Europe
Government Type: Constitutional Monarchy
Population: 5.2 million
Three largest cities: Copenhagen (Capital), Arhus and Odense
Currency: Krone

55.   The Romanovs (1613-1917)

56.   Prussian.
Catherine the Great was born in 1729. Married in 1744, she ruled
Russia from 1762 to 1796.

57. Simon Bolivar

58. Between Russia and the allied powers of England, France, Sardinia and Turkey.

59. Saladin, the Sultan of Egypt.
He brought about the Third Crusade by capturing Jerusalem in 1187. Saladin signed a truce with Richard I of England in 1192.

60. The International Red Cross

61. The Crimean War

62. Potato.
The lack of potatos caused the deaths of one million people. A greater number emigrated, mostly to the United States.

63. Germany, Italy and Japan

64. Catherine of Aragon was the first wife of Henry VIII of England and the daughter of Ferdinand and Isabella of Spain.

65. The Manchu dynasty

66. The League of Nations

67. Napoleon of France

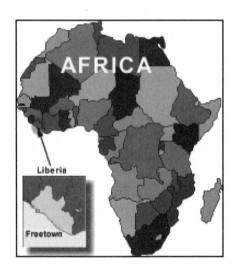

68. Constantine, King of Hellenas

69. Freetown in Liberia (Africa)

70. The Incas, the Aztecs and the Mayans

71. Ra

72. Aeneas

73. India and South Korea

74. Adolph Hitler

75. The Battle of Gettysburg

Literature

Answers

....

Literature Answers

1. *Mahabharata* (India)

2. Baroness Orczy

3. *Merchant of Venice*

4. Lewis Carroll, the pseudonym of Charles Lutwidge Dodgson.

5. Desdemona

6. Homer.
    The *Iliad* is the story of the seige of Troy and the *Odyssey* is the story of Odysseus's adventures.

7. Mary Ann Evans

8. W. Somerset Maugham

9. Sir Walter Scott

10. Jean Jacques Rousseau

11. Charles Dickens

12. "The Brook" by Alfred Lord Tennyson.

13. Miguel de Cervantes Saavedra

14. Edinburgh, Scotland in December, 1768.

15. *What You Will*

16. Jacob and Wilhelm.

17. Samuel Langhorne Clemens

18. *Twelfth Night* by William Shakespeare.

19. Peter Ilich Tchaikovsky

20. Brutus in *Julius Caesar* (Act V, Scene 5).

Voltaire
(1694-1778)

Voltaire is considered to be the greatest French writer and philosopher of his time. His writings and philosophical ideas had tremendous impact on the French Revolution. Voltaire's outspoken nature forced him to leave France several times. He spend the last years of his life in Paris.

Johann Wolfgang von Goethe
(1749-1832)

Goethe, a German poet and dramatist, wrote his first two plays while studying law at Leipzig. During the next several years, he wrote his famous plays and poems while working at the Weimar court in Strasbourgh.

Jules Verne
(1828-1905)

Jules Verne was a famous French novelist who wrote several adventure books.

21.   Voltaire (French)

22.   T. E. Lawrence

23.   Johann Wolfgang von Goethe

24.   Macduff

25.   Rupert Brooke

26.   Egypt

27.   Jules Verne

28.   *The Tempest*

29.   Sir John Falstaff

30.   His own name – Arthur Conan Doyle

31.   Alfred Lord Tennyson

32.   Thomas Stearns Eliot.

33.   *The Old Man and the Sea*

34. Jean-Paul Sartre and Albert Camus.

35. William Golding

36. Silver

37. Margaret Mitchell

38. Denmark

39. Friday

40. Brobdingnagians

41. *The Mystery of Edwin Drood*

42. *Sohrab and Rustum*

43. George Bernard Shaw

44. Gilbert K. Chesterton

45. Morgan le Fay

46. Every Roman citizen

47. Henri Albert Guy de Maupassant.
Maupasssant is famous for his short stories and novels.

48. A philosophy that states that the goal of a human being should be a life of calm pleasure, serenity and cultural awareness.

49. Hank Ketcham

50. A roc.

51. Twenty years.

52. Alfred Lord Tennyson

53. *Lorna Doone*

54. *The Epic of Gilgamesh*

55. The first, second and fifth rhyme have three beats each, and the third and fourth rhyme have two beats each.

56. Tennessee Williams

57. Norris and Ross McWhirter compiled the first *Guiness Book of World Records*.

58. A short comic play accompanied by music.

59. Maxim Gorky

60. Bathos: sudden descent from the exalted to the ridiculous.
Pathos: awakening feelings of sympathy and tenderness.

61. *Macbeth* by Shakespeare.

62. *The Sound of Music*

63. Mexico

64. Louis Untermeyer

65. Stephen Crane

66. *Rubaiyat.*
Originally *Ruibaiyat* was composed in Persian. Edward Fitzgerald translated it into English.

67. Alexander Dumas

68. Sir Arthur Conan Doyle

69. Rudyard Kipling.
The sentence appeared in Kipling's famous narrative titled *Ballad*

of East and West.

70.   Victor Hugo

71.   John Goldwater

72.   Stan Lee and Flor Dery.

73.   An antonym is a word that means the opposite of another word. For example, the word 'hot' is the antonym for the word 'cold'.

74.   Walt Whitman

75.   Murasaki Shikibu

Cross Word Puzzle
General – Answer

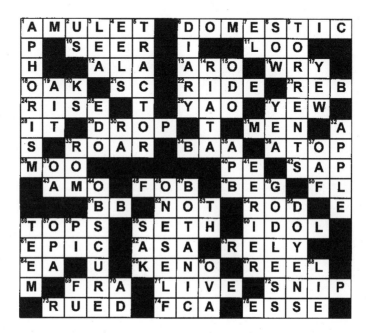

Science

Answers

································

Science Answers

1.   Alexander Graham Bell.

2.   John Napier in 1614.

3.   Sir J. J. Thompson.
      Thompson was well-known for his work regarding the mathematical theory of electricity. He received the Noble Prize in Physics in 1906. Thomson also served as the President of the Royal Society of London.

4.   Ronald Ross.
      Ross was awarded the Noble Prize for Medicine in 1902 for his discovery.

5.   The femur or the thigh bone.

6.   Guglielmo Marconi on June 22nd, 1896.

7.   Benjamin Franklin in 1752.

8.   There are no nerves in the nails.

9.   John Loud in 1888.

10.   Dr. Alexander Fleming

11.   Aerodynamics

12.   Sir Fredrick Banting and J. Macleod

13.   Niels Bohr

14.   A chemical or nonchemical substance that accelerates reactions without undergoing any changes itself.

15.   Convex or diverging mirror.
       Convex mirrors form a smaller image, allowing for a wider view.

16.   Karl Scheele in 1771.

17.   Mass is the quantity of matter contained in a body, while weight is the force of attraction of the earth on a given mass.

Benjamin Franklin
(1706-1790)

Benjamin Franklin was a scientist, an inventor, a diplomat, writer, a painter, and a philosopher. But did you know that Franklin also coined some of the often used phrases of today? Here are some examples of his work:

"Early to bed and early to rise, makes a man healthy, wealthy, and wise."

"God helps them that help themselves."

"Necessity never made a good bargain."

18. Laughing gas

19. Artery

20. William Harvey of England.

21. Sir Humphry Davy in 1808.

22. Lunik II on September 14th, 1959.

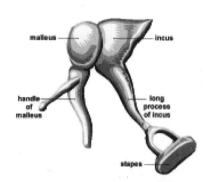

23. Gluteus Maximus or the buttock muscle.

24. 9.80665 metres/sec^2 or 32.3 feet/sec^2.

25. Stapes or stirrup bone located in the middle ear.

26. 35,000,000° C.
    The sun uses up to 10 million atoms of hydrogen per second thus, providing a luminosity of 3 X 10^{27} candle power per square inch.

The Middle Ear Bones

The ear is divided into three major areas: outer, middle, and inner ear. The midle ear, also called the tympanic cavity, is spanned by the three smallest bones in the body. These bones are named for their shapes. They are the **malleus**, or hammer; the **incus**, or anvil; and the **stapes**, or stirrup.

27. Gregor Mendel of Austria.

28. Three

29. Four

30. The ionosphere

31. Olaus Roemer.
While an assistant at the Royal Observatory, Paris, Roemer estimated the approximate velocity of light through observations of the eclipse of satellites of Jupiter.

FYI FYI FYI FYI

How many noble gases are there?

There are six noble gases: Helium (He), Neon (Ne), Argon (Ar), Krypton (Kr), Xenon (Xe), and Radon (Rn). Noble gases lack the ability to react with other elements.

32. Galvanometer is used for the detection of small amounts of currents.

33. Carbon

34. The mariner's compass has 32 points.

35. Boyle's Law states that if the temperature of an ideal gas remains constant then its volume varies inversely with its pressure.

36. Thiamine

37. Kinematics

38. Vinegar

Kinematics – the study of motion.

39. Eight minutes and 19 seconds (499 seconds)

40. Tetanus

41. A. H. Becquerel of France.

42. Limestone composed entirely or partly of calcite or domomite crystals.

43. Morpheus
Morphine is the drug.

44. An old orbital communication satellite used to relay live trans-Atlantic TV broadcasts.

45. Escape velocity is the minimum velocity required by an object in order to escape from the attarction of gravity.

46. Air is removed from an electric bulb to prevent oxidation of the metallic filamant by atmospheric oxygen.

47. The spectroscope

48. Lipase is the enzyme involved in the breakdown of fats to their constituent fatty acids and alcohols.

49. Proxima Centauri.
    Proxima Centauri is approximately 4.3 light years away. However, all heavenly bodies are in constant motion. As a result, it is expected that by the year 11,800 the nearest star will be Barnard's Star.

Stars Nearest To The Earth	
1. Proxima Centauri	4.22 light years away
2. Alpha Centauri	4.35 light years away
3. Barnard's Star	5.98 light years away
4. Wolf 359	7.75 light years away
5. Lalande 21185	8.22 light years away

50. The Great Bear and the Plough

51. Adrenalin

52. 15°

53. The Theory of Evolution.
Charles Darwin was one of the foremost proponents of the
evolutionary theory with regard to the origin of man. He authored
an authorative book on evolution called *The Origin of the Species*,
which was published in 1859.

54. Diseases related to tooth decay.

55. Iron

56. Polysaccharides are complex sugars composed of multiple units of
simple sugars.

57. Bats

58. A scalene triangle whose three sides and interior angles are all
different from each other.

59. A spider

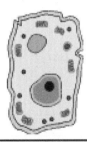

PARTS OF A CELL

Plasma Membrane – regulates what materials are transported in and out of the cell.
Nucleus – directs the activities of the cell.
Ribosome – is the site of protein synthesis.
Endoplasmic reticulum – is a continuous channel that extends into many regions of the cell.
Rough ER – channels with ribosomes.
Smooth ER – channels without ribosomes.
Golgi Bodies: – stacks of flattened sacs, which also participate in protein synthesis.
Mitochondria – often referred to as the "powerhouse" of the cell because they provide us with energy molecules.
Lysosomes – tiny sacs which release digestive enzymes to break down worn-out organelles.
Centrioles – produce special fibers called microtubules.
Cytoskeleton – a network of fibers which participate in cellular division and movement.
Microtubules – fibers which are involved in cell movement.

60. Panda

61. Raisin

62. Refraction of light in the atmosphere

63. Usually the salivary or parotid glands in front of the ears are inflamed.

64. Haversian canals are microscopic channels in the bone through which blood vessels innervate various parts of the bone.

65. Nitrogen

66. Rod shaped
     Bacillus is Latin for rod.

67. James Ritty in 1879.

68. A cytologist studies cells.

69. About ten days.

70. Venus

71.   Skull

72.   The individual suffers from color blindness.

73.   Polaris (the Pole Star or North Star) helps navigators identify the North. Polaris is the brightest star in the Little Bear (Ursa Minor) constellation. It always remains visible in the northern hemisphere and is never more than 1° from due North.

74.   The feet

75.   Ballistics

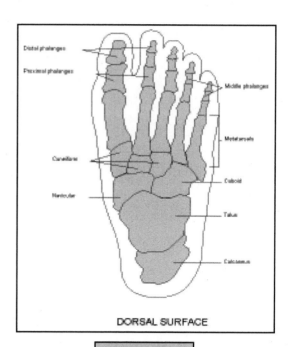

A Typical Feet

General Topics

Answers

....

General Topics Answers

1. The Pentagon in Washington, D.C.
    Completed in 1943, Pentagon is a five story building with a floor area of 605,000 square meters.

2. The statue of Motherland in Russia.
    It is nearly 270 feet tall. The statue was designed to commemorate the victory of Stalingrad (1942-43).

3. 1.151 miles per hour or 1.84 km per hour.

4. Dag Hammarskjold, the late U.N. Secretary-General.

5. 1901.
    The Noble Prize is named after Alfred Noble who invented dynamite. Sweden awards the Noble Prize annually on December 10.

6. Atlantic Sailfish

7.   Suriname

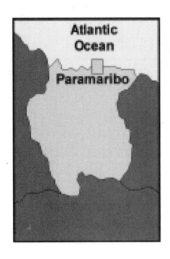

Suriname
Independence Day: November 25
Location: Northeastern coast of South America
Government Type: Civilian Rule
Population: 450,000
Capital: Paramaribo
Currency: Suriname Guilder

8.   The Huey Long Bridge in Metairie, Louisiana.

9.   Surveyor-I

10.   4.53 liters

11.   The leader of the opposition party.

12.   Lotus

13.   376,285 km (surface to surface)

14. Sea of Tranquility

15. Russia

16. The Hague

17. Plato

18. President
    The Chancellor is the head of the government.

19. The Great Wall of China, build during the
    reign of Shih Huangti, is 2150 miles long.

The Great Wall of China
The only man-made object
visible from the outer space.

20. December 10

21. Mt. Kilimanjaro (6012 meters high)

22. Vijayalakshmi Pandit of India.

23. Geneva, Switzerland

24. Gross National Product

25. Roald Amundsen of Norway.
    He reached the North Pole on December 4, 1911.

26.   Vasco da Gama (Portuguese) in 1498.

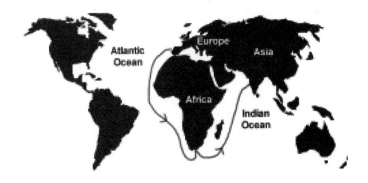

The sea route followed by Vasco da Gama from Portugal to India around the Cape of Good Hope (located at the southern tip of Africa).

27.   The official residence of the President of France. Originally built for Louis d'Auvergne in 1718 and bought by Madame de Pompadour in 1753, it was the residence of French kings till 1848.

28.   Auguste Rodin

29.   Inventing a system of reading for the blind (Braille system).

30.   Olive tree.

31.   From *Januarius* (Latin) after Janus, the two-faced Roman God of Doorways.

32.   Sextant is used to measure the altitude of the sun.

Time Out!

How is it going?

Are your brain cells working overtime?

Hang in there…
You are almost done.

33. Sir William Lawrence Bragg (U.K.) at the age of 25.

34. Switzerland

35. Swedish Krona

36. July and August.
Named after the Roman Emperors Julius Caesar and
Augustus Caesar.

37. Cuckoo

38. Cartography

Julius Caesar
*Emperor of the
Roman Republic*

First Five Roman Emperors	
1. Julius Caesar	48 BC-27BC
2. Augustus	27 BC-14 BC
3. Tiberius	14 BC-AD 37
4. Caligula	AD 37-AD 41
5. Claudius	AD 41-AD 54

39. Stratus

40. Chaelie Chaplin.

41. Agoraphobia

42. Silviculturists grow trees.

43. The Pope

44. Flax

45. The Colossus, a bronze statue of Apollo.

46. The name means "Haven of Peace".

47. Challenger Deep located southwest of Guam in the Pacific Ocean.

48. Quirinal Palace

49. Belgium

50. Leonardo da Vinci

51. Sir Lancelot

52. Minimum: Two
Maximum: Five

53. The *Victoria* used on Magellan's expedition around the world in 1521-22.

54. The tulip

55. Spanish

56. The measurement of angles.

57. The Mastiff and the Bulldog.

Leonardo da Vinci
(1452–1519)

Leonardo was born on April 15, 1452, in the small Tuscan town of Vinci, near Florence. The Mona Lisa, Leonardo da Vinci's most famous work, is well known for its mastery of technical innovations and the mysteriousness of its legendary smiling subject. As a scientist Leonardo was well ahead of all his contemporaries. A master of art, sciences and technology, Leonardo da Vinci has left a lasting legacy behind through his works.

58. Rocket fuel carries its own oxygen while jet fuel obtains oxygen from the atmosphere.

59. London, England

IMAGES FROM

GREECE

60. Athens, Greece

61. Pegasus.

62. On the shores off the Straits of Gibraltar.

63. Hawaii

64. A large horned mountain goat.

65. A sea bird.

66. Paris, son of Priam.

67. In the Louvre in Paris.

68. Mt. Vesuvius

69. Mars, the Roman God of War.

70. Portugal

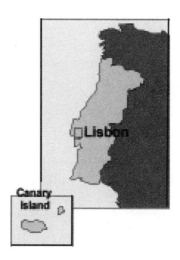

Portugal

Independence Day: October 5

Location: On the Iberian Peninsula in southwestern Europe

Government Type: Republic

Population: 11 million

Three largest cities: Lisbon (Capital), Porto and Amadora

Currency: Escudo

71. La Scala is an opera house in Milan, Italy.

72. Photography means "writing with light".

73. Metal strings, strung over a shallow closed box, are struck with two hammers.

74. Jupiter Symphony

75. Helios

76.   Prima donna

77.   Vincent van Gogh

78.   Italy (Bartolomeo Cristoforie, 1709).

FYI FYI FYI FYI

How is Turn Iwatani?

Turn Iwatani (Japanese) designed and created one of the world's most popular video game called *Pac-Man*. He was twenty seven years old and worked for a Japanese video game maker at the time.

79.   Johann Strauss

80.   Impressionism

81.   Mercury (Roman)
Hermes (Greek)

82.   John Bull

83. Minerva

84. Vishnu

85. Castor and Pollux.

86. The Brontes

WHAT'S IN A NAME?		
God	**Roman**	**Greek**
God of Sea	Neptune	Poseidon
Goddess of Love	Venus	Aphrodite
Goddess of Wisdom	Minerva	Athena
God of the Sun	Apollo	Apollo
God of Wine	Bacchus	Dionysus

87. Beethoven was born in Bonn and wrote nine symphonies.

88. The tomb of the Unknown Soldier.

89. Wife of William Shakespeare.
Anne Hathaway was eight years older that her husband. She married Shakespeare at the age of 26 in 1582.

90. Hafiz

91. Goa is a small Tibetan antelope found on the Tibetan Plateau.

92. Scotland

93. Excalibur

94. Sweden

95.   J. Bardeen, W. H. Brattain and W. Shockley (U.S.A)

96.   The House of Windsor

97.   W. Judson (U.S.A.)

98.   Ferdinand Magellan

99.   Belize

100. Leonard Spencer

101. Mozart

102. Bolivia and Paraguay.

103. Promethium named after Prometheus.

104. Tokyo, Japan

105. Martin Luther

106. Jean Francois Millet (France)

107. Thursday is named after the Scandinavian god Thor and Friday after Frigga, the wife of Odin.

108. Shangra La

109. Amman

110. Abraham Lincoln

111. Israel

112. Chaos

113. South Carolina

114. Mother Theresa

115. Green

Cross Word Puzzle
Business Leaders
Answer

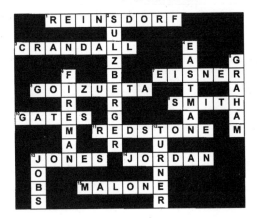

Cross Word Puzzle
General Puzzle – Answer

Internet Search Engines

The World Wide Web (WWW) is a great place to look for trivia questions. Hundreds of trivia related web sites have popped up on the Internet in the last few months. Use the following search engines to sort through hundreds of sites to find the one that interests you. Have fun surfing the Net!

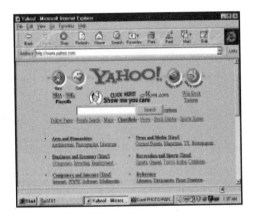

www.yahoo.com

Key Search Words:

Trivia
Knowledge games
brain twisters

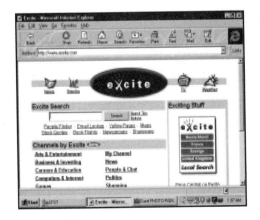

www.excite.com

Key Search Words:

Trivia
Knowledge games

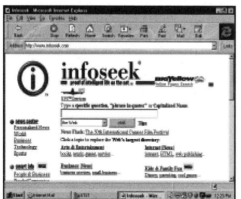

www.infoseek.com

Key Search Words:

Trivia
Knowledge games

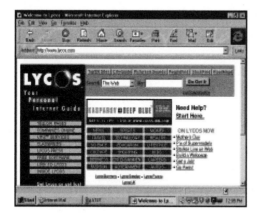

www.lycos.com

Key Search Words:

Trivia
Knowledge games

Other Trivia Related Web Sites

Family Resource Center
http://www.shop-utopia.com/reference/

Steve Younis' Web of Wonder
http://www.geocities.com/EnchantedForest/5071.index.html

Talk City's Games Galore
http://www.talkcity.com

Trivia Room
http://www.europa.com

Cellar Quiz
http://www.celebs.net

Riddle du Jour
http://www.dujour.com